Suzanne Beedell is the author of
books covering topics as diverse as dinghy
sailing and home winemaking. She currently
lives in Deal, Kent, in a house overlooking
the sea, where she and her family have much
enjoyed all the recipe testing involved in
compiling this delicious cookery book!

Also by Suzanne Beedell in Sphere Books:

WINE MAKING AND HOME BREWING

The Curry Cook Book

SUZANNE BEEDELL

SPHERE BOOKS LIMITED
30/32 Gray's Inn Road, London WC1X 8JL

First published in Great Britain by
Sphere Books Ltd 1979
Reprinted 1980, 1984
Copyright © Suzanne Beedell 1979

TRADE
MARK

Set in Intertype Times

Printed in Great Britain by
Hunt Barnard Printing Ltd.,
Aylesbury, Bucks.

Contents

Author's Note

This book has been a joint effort: the recipes have been tried on families and friends by me and by Ginette Leach, who has helped greatly with the research and the work of putting the book together. My thanks to her and to the involuntary food tasters.

S. M. B.

Introduction

No one ever reads introductions so this will be very short!

Even if you have never made a curry in your life, you could soon become an excellent curry cook: provided you begin at the beginning of this book and work through it to the end. I have quite deliberately not been slavish about quantities, materials, or methods, and some of the early recipes are very basic indeed, but nevertheless I believe that any Western cook will find herein many excellent recipes that must add vastly to his/her repertoire and reputation.

Additionally there is a lot of information about curry terms – so that you need no longer be flummoxed by menus in curry restaurants – and help with planning curry meals and parties. Everything, in fact, that you might wish to know to be well informed on the subject, without going deeply into technicalities or making a mystic art out of something which is really very simple, provided you are prepared to take a little time and trouble.

I have probably horrified the purists, but I did not write this book for purists. I write for people who enjoy their food, enjoy feeding others, and enjoy cooking.

Curry Menu Planner

Throughout the book recipes are graded as 'beginners''
'intermediate' and 'advanced'. In the list below the recipes
are set out in categories, ie 'Soup', 'Fish' etc, and in their
grades.

Just look in the different categories to find a recipe for
cooking the food you have in mind and pick a beginners',
intermediate or advanced recipe as you wish.

There is an Index at the end of the book to help you to
find specific things if you cannot find them in the lists below.

SOUPS

RICE

DAHL

BREADS, CRISPS AND BATTERS

EGGS

SAUCES

Intermediate

Lamb Kebabs	80
Minced Lamb Kebabs	80

Advanced

Special Lamb Pilau	121
Lamb Pilau	125
Lamb and Chicken Pilau	127
Nutty Mutton Curry	130
Lamb Biriani	131

PORK

Beginners'

Pork in Curry Sauce	38
Pork Tandoori	39
Special Pork Tandoori	39
Pork Vindaloo	59

Intermediate

Diced Pork in Coconut Sauce	81
Pork Sate	83
Spiced Spare Ribs	84
Sweet and Sour Pork Balls (Chasnidarh)	84

Advanced

Pork, Shrimp and Fried Rice (Nasi Goreng)	123

POULTRY

Beginners'

Left-over Chicken Curry	36
Duck Curry	45
Legs of Chicken in Curry Sauce	42
Chinese Curry Chicken	43
Sweet Chicken Curry	44
Chicken Kebabs in Sate Sauce	44
Chicken Vindaloo	57

VEGETABLES

ACCOMPANIMENTS

CHUTNEYS

DESSERTS, FRUIT AND ICES

17

Sweet Rice

DRINKS

18

Chapter 1

*ABOUT CURRY, WEIGHTS
AND MEASURES, COOKING
HEAT, UTENSILS, GLOSSARY
OF NAMES AND TERMS,
FOOD MATERIALS OTHER
THAN SPICES, OILS AND
FATS, SPICES, AND HERBS
SAUCES AND SEASONINGS*

About Curry

The very first thing that the beginner curry cook and eater must do is to get rid of a few preconceived ideas about eating. We are so used to meat and two veg, or chips with everything, that it is difficult for us to think in other terms. We go for a main ingredient; meat, fish, poultry, plus potatoes, green vegetables, root vegetables, and sometimes salad, and the whole meal builds up on affinities like mint sauce with lamb, sage and onion with pork, Yorkshire pudding with beef.

Curries are absolutely different. I'm using the word curry in its widest sense to cover all the Indian and Asian varieties of spiced food, not necessarily red-hot. There are, for us at any rate, no rules. Anything can be eaten with anything. Try an Indonesian Rijst-Tafel in an Indo-Chinese restaurant in Holland and you will probably be served with at least twenty different dishes for two people. In Britain we are used to the many varieties of Chinese dishes (not necessarily curried). Having said this, it must also be said that there are many excellent one-dish curries which can be made very easily and served with just one or two accompaniments.

So never let anyone tell you that you cannot serve this with that, or those with these. Another great thing about curry cookery is that it is almost impossible to make an irreparable mistake, other than that of putting in so much chilli that the food blows the tops off everyone's heads, and brings tears to the eyes even of the man with the most utterly ruined palate!

No one would ever claim that the flavours of curry spices are delicate, so a bit more or a bit less is not going to ruin the food. For the same reason unavailable spices can be left out or replaced by something else.

Notwithstanding what I said in the last paragraph, the use of individual spices rather than made-up curry powder, DOES alter flavours, and as you learn the art, is definitely to be recommended.

There are variations in the curries, in the way they are cooked and served, in the ingredients which are used in the balance of spices. So many Indonesian curries contain coconut milk (santan), for instance, yet very few Indian curries use coconut other than as an accompaniment. However, for our Western purposes, there is no need at all to divide the recipes up country by country. I have Anglicised everything, with Indian words in brackets, and where ingredients are not obtainable except in specialised shops in the main cities, have used our nearest substitute.

All recipes will provide four to six servings according to appetite unless otherwise stated.

Weights and Measures

Metrication, which was supposed to standardise weights

and measures, has merely served to confuse even further an already complicated subject. When considering recipes in which quantities are crucial, things become very difficult both for cookery writer and for cook, because the book may be read by people used to metric measurements in kilograms and litres and their subdivisions, to Imperial measures in lbs, ozs, gallons and pints, or to American measurements in cups, or spoonsful in various sizes.

Luckily, in curry cookery, absolutely exact measurements are not crucial, and in fact within the broad limits of quantities given, experimentation – a little more or a little less of this and that – merely produces endless permutations of flavour.

Therefore in this book quantities have been given in pounds and grams, in pints and decilitres, and sometimes in ounces where this is inescapable, but usually in LEVEL teaspoons (tspn), dessertspoons (dssrtspn) and tablespoons (tbspn), because this is the most convenient way to handle small quantities of spices, herbs, flour, butter, oil, etc. The American cup measurement has not been used in the recipes.

There is also a difference between the American standard tablespoon and the British standard tablespoon, but for the purposes of this book it is NOT the exact amounts which are important, but the proportions. The tablespoons, dessertspoons, and teaspoons with which you measure your spices etc, will probably be the ordinary ones that you use in your house everyday, and there is nothing wrong with these. Just fill the spoon to very slightly more than level, but not heaped.

I have not, therefore, included complicated weights and measures conversion tables; they are not necessary, and you will learn to cook curries as the Eastern cook does, sometimes altering the proportions to suit your taste. This applies particularly to chilli powder, to suit the heat tolerance of your palate; garlic, which may be disliked by many British people; and coconut, which is a flavour not enjoyed by some, and which is very pervasive once added to a curry.

Aniseed and mixed spice powders containing it, used by Chinese cooks, can also be unpleasant to our taste if over-done.

Cooking Temperatures

The broad subdivisions of hot, medium and low, with perhaps very low sometimes, are all that is necessary. You are not making a cake or a soufflé with subtle rising temperature; just cooking various things as described in the recipes. Fast overcooking is possibly the greatest danger to curries, particularly when frying – it is very easy to burn onions, for instance. Slow cooking will almost never hurt a curry. In fact except where ingredients must not be reduced to a mushy pulp (vegetables generally) slow cooking without much stirring improves the flavour of a curry. The modern electric casserole which can be left safely all day or all night to slow-cook food is absolutely excellent for many curries, as long as they do not actually contain rice, which should never be overcooked.

Utensils

A heavy frying pan is essential, and a couple of heavy-based saucepans will be needed for cooking rice and simmering. Casseroles and oven dishes with lids are essential, and a good steamer is extremely useful. Drum-shaped bamboo steamers to fit the tops of standard size saucepans can be bought cheaply from Chinese food shops: Cheoong Lins in Tower Street, London W1, stock absolutely everything of this kind. These steamers are marvellous for cooking vegetables, but not for rice as the holes in the bottom are too big.

As mentioned on page 157, metal serving dishes of all shapes and sizes are excellent for curries because they retain heat, and a good hotplate is also extremely useful.

A really good sharp cook's knife and some spoons in various sizes for measuring and stirring, a fish slice for turning things in frying pans, and some kebab skewers, are all you need, along with a chopping board and a good

22

grater and perhaps a patent chopper for vegetables.

Of course a good electric mincing machine and a blender are very useful, and the blender can save hours of work pounding things in mortars or forcing them through sieves.

From all this you will appreciate that curry cookery is not difficult. It was developed as peasant cookery in the Far East, using local spices, meat and vegetables, and the utensils and charcoal fires used were of the very simplest. Modern cookery schools and the like have not, fortunately, succeeded in altering all this in any significant way. Cordon Bleu is never a term applied to curry cookery. It is interesting that except for Holland and Britain, who had huge Empires in the Far East, no European country produces good curries as part of its cuisine, certainly not France, which has otherwise indisputably the best cuisine in the world. It is true that the best curry restaurants in Holland and Britain are run by Indo-Chinese (in Holland) and Indians and Pakistanis (in Britain) but a lot of curry is cooked and eaten in the home in both countries.

Glossary of Curry Names and Terms

For readers who frequent Indian, Pakistani, Indonesian and Chinese restaurants, all the following terms may well be familiar. But for others it can be very useful to know them – or some of them – not only for cooking purposes, but also to be knowledgeable when eating out, and to avoid mistakes when ordering food. For the purpose of this list, no classification has been made of separate languages and the terms are listed alphabetically. Only in the definitions is the country of origin sometimes mentioned. The page references are to recipes for that particular type of curry.

Aviyal is a southern Indian name given to mixtures of vegetables and seeds. The spices and seeds are fried, then the other vegetables added and cooked in a purée of coconut and water. (See page 101)

Bhajjis is the general name given to Indian vegetable dishes, which are usually fried.

Bhugia. This is any vegetable dish cooked without water. Many different vegetables can be used and care must be taken when cooking so that they do not end up too dry and too hot. (See page 96)

Bhurtas are mixed vegetable and spice dishes.

Birianis differ from other rice dishes in three ways. They are always yellowed by saffron or turmeric, contain cumin and coriander seeds, and whole peppercorns and large black cardamoms. They are much richer than pilau, and should contain twice as much meat or fish as rice. (See page 131)

Blachan is a paste made with prawns. It is a basic flavouring used all over South East Asia. (See page 30)

Bombay Duck is a species of cured, dried fish which is heated in the oven and when quite crisp, broken up and sprinkled over the curry.

Chaat is the name given to any fresh fruit salad spiced with chillies, red peppers, lemon juice and salt. (See page 147)

Chakees are made from mixed vegetables, usually boiled.

Chapatties. Unleavened flat bread pancakes eaten with curries. (See page 103)

Chasnidarh is food cooked or finished in a sweet-sour sauce made from sugar and vinegar, or lemon or lime juice. Pork, duck, lamb, veal and fish, as well as bananas or cherries, or vegetables such as turnip, carrot or beetroot are all suitable for cooking in this style. (See page 84)

Dal, Dahl or *Dhall* is part of the staple diet in India. There are many varieties, made from lentils or split peas cooked to the consistency of thick sauce with added onions, chillis and turmeric and eaten either just with boiled rice, or as a side dish with hot curry. (See page 68)

Dopiazah, Do Peezah or *Do Puaza* is a dish which has a great deal of onion in it, with amounts of onion at least equal to the amount of meat, and up to twice the weight of the meat. The onions are always divided into two lots, the first half being fried with the meat, and the second being cut finely and added raw when the meat is half cooked.

The two onion preparations give an interesting taste with different textures.

Foogath is a dish which uses pre-cooked vegetables and extra spices and is cooked until everything is very dry.

Ghee is the universal Indian cooking fat. It is clarified butter with the impurities removed. It will heat to a higher temperature than other cooking oils or fats, so it is perfect to release the flavour of spices and for very crisp cooking. (See page 29)

Halwa, Halva or *Hulva*. This is a traditional dessert from northern India and is rather sweet for Western tastes, and can be made with a great variety of ingredients. (See page 142)

Jallebi. These are yeasty crisp buns, but are terribly sweet to Western taste, and to be really nice they must be freshly made.

Kababs, Kebabs or *Khababs* are meat and vegetables heavily spiced, cut into chunks or minced, and skewered. They are cooked over an open fire or charcoal, or can be grilled. (See page 40)

Korma. This is meat or vegetables braised in water, stock, yoghurt or cream, and cooked, depending on the recipe, until the liquid becomes a glaze, or a thick sauce, or even until it is quite dry and flakey. (See page 87)

Madras Curry. A very hot curry! Many Madrassi curries are rather thin and watery.

Molee is the name given to food cooked in thick coconut milk.

Nam Pak is prawn, blachan and chilli sauce served with raw vegetables and sharp fruit. It is usually served in a bowl set in the middle of mixed fruit and vegetables, all beautifully prepared, as this is an essential part of the menu in Thailand.

Nasi is the Indonesian word for rice, hence Nasi Goreng etc. (See page 123)

Pakora. A special batter made from gram flour with yoghurt to moisten it, and filled with sliced vegetables or fruit, aubergine being one of the most successful. It is fried, just

25

like any fritter, in hot oil and served either as a snack or with curry. (See page 72)

Palak is anything cooked with spinach.

Panch Phora is a combination of five spices in equal quantities.

Panggang. This is a South East Asian way of preparing a chicken by severing the whole bird down the sternum and bending it back, breaking the ribs at the back. The legs are pinned level with the tail by inserting a skewer across the back of the chicken, and it is cooked in this flattened-out position.

Parathas. A type of bread to be eaten with curry. (See page 70)

Phirni is a kind of blancmange with almonds and pistachios.

Pilau. A curry cooked this way always has rice as its base, contains dried fruit such as sultanas, and nuts, and is prepared in butter. (See page 125)

Poppadums. A very crisp 'biscuit' eaten with curries.

Puris, Poorees. A type of bread. (See page 70)

Raeta is the general term for any vegetables or fruit cooked in yoghurt to go with a hot curry. It is served cold. (See page 106)

Samosa is a kind of Indian Cornish pasty, being made from a special pastry case, usually containing potatoes, peas and minced meat. (See page 75)

Santan is coconut milk, which is an essential ingredient in many Indonesian curries and other recipes. (See page 31)

Satay, Sate is a kebab from Malaya: steak or chicken cut into cubes, put on a skewer and grilled, and served with a special sauce poured over and eaten with pieces of rice cake, or plain boiled rice. (See page 110)

Tandoori. This name originally came from the high clay ovens in which this dish was cooked on a spit. In a recipe or on a menu it means that the meat or chicken has been slashed and then put into a cooked sauce or marinade of spices for several hours before cooking. Tandoori food should be grilled on an open fire or barbecue or an electric spit. It can be baked in an oven, but will lose its crisp finish. (See page 39)

Vindaloo. In many Indian restaurants this means it is the hottest curry on the menu, but really vindaloo is a method of cooking where the meat (usually pork) is marinated for twenty-four hours, and this marinade always contains vinegar. When making vindaloo at home, the amount of chilli can be adjusted to taste. (See page 55)

Materials Other Than Spices for Curries

The beauty of curries is that they can be made from absolutely any cut of meat or fish or poultry, and it is not necessary to buy expensive cuts of meat. The very fact that most curries require and benefit from long slow cooking means that meat which might otherwise be tough, becomes very tender.

If you buy ready minced meat from the butcher it will contain rather too much fat, and this must be eliminated before making the curry by putting the meat in a casserole, breaking it up with a fork, and cooking it for $\frac{3}{4}$ hour in a medium to slow oven. The fat can then be poured off and the meat will have been improved by some precooking. If you are using a recipe which requires lean minced beef, uncooked, then you must buy some lean beef without fat or gristle and either mince it at home or persuade the butcher to do it for you. All kinds of once-cooked meat and poultry, remains of roasts, etc are fine for curries and can be substituted for fresh meat, and cooking time reduced accordingly. However, NEVER just warm up once-cooked meat or poultry, it must be heated right up to boiling point and simmered for a few minutes at some point during the making of the curry.

Cooked chicken – either whole or pieces, which can be bought from most butchers nowadays – is excellent for currying as it will not take so long to be cooked through as raw chicken. It is very useful for making quick curries as the pieces only need to be covered in almost any concoction of curry spices in the form of a sauce and simmered for $\frac{1}{2}$

27

hour or so to absorb some of the flavours. The skin, if the poultry has been precooked, can be left on if liked. (See recipes pages 42–78)

It is best to use fresh firm fish for curries. Prawns and shrimps may be fresh, frozen, dried or tinned, but tinned shrimps and prawns tend to break up and disappear, and should be thoroughly drained before use, because the canned liquid is very salty.

Vegetables and pulses for curries may be fresh, frozen, tinned or dried, although except for tinned tomatoes and tinned pease pudding (for dahl) tinned vegetables have too much flavouring added in the canning processes and also tend to go mushy when cooked in mixed dishes. Fresh vegetables are always best; frozen are a good substitute.

Oils and Fats for Curries

Any good vegetable oil is suitable for cooking curry. Having said that, I must point out that coconut oil, olive oil, peanut oil, sesame oil, sunflower oil and mustard oil all impart different flavours, and if you do use them, they can improve the curry. Mustard oil is frequently used for fish curries, peanut oil for Indonesian curries, especially those which will be served with sate sauce, and coconut oil for curries which contain coconut.

Ordinary butter is fine for most curries, although if you use salted butter remember to reduce salt in the recipe a little. Unsalted butter will do; it can be mixed half and half with oil, when it will not burn so easily. Margarine and lard can be mixed half and half with oil, but impart no flavour and should only be used if you have nothing else. Dripping is rarely used for curries.

Most of the recipes in this book specify oil or butter, but in fact Eastern cooks, particularly Indian, Pakistani or Sri Lankan, would use ghee. This is clarified butter made from buffalo milk. It has a higher burning point than other oils so it is perfect for frying and searing meat and getting the best out of curry spices. It also keeps much longer (in fact indefinitely) than ordinary butter, especially in a hot climate.

28

It can be bought in tins from Indian grocers in this country, but is very, very expensive.

It is easy enough to make your ghee although of cows' not buffalo butter! Put 2 lbs/1kg of best unsalted butter into a heavy saucepan and melt it. It MUST NOT BURN, so cook it over a very low heat or with an asbestos mat above the flame. Keep it just below the point at which it bubbles, and skim off any impurities or scum. Continue for an hour, by which time the water content should have evaporated and impurities sunk to the bottom. Allow the ghee to cool for 5 minutes, then strain it through several thicknesses of butter muslin tied over the top of a pudding basin. Pour it into clean jars, cover and store in a cool place.

Spices and Herbs, Sauces and Seasonings

The spices and herbs are listed in alphabetical order, but I have marked with a star those which are essential if you are to develop your curry cooking methods. Almost all the spices can be bought in powdered form, and although the purists say you should buy the seeds and grind them for yourself, I think that this is asking a lot of busy British cooks! Unless you are going to make your own curry powder blends and keep them in screw-top jars, it seems rather pointless when all the spices can be bought freshly ground, from delicatessen and specialist food shops. These can be found in all our cities and in many big towns. Even quite small towns have delicatessens these days, and if they do not stock the spices, chutneys, curry powders, and pastes that you want, they should be able to get them for you. There are only a few wholesalers supplying these things, and the delicatessen is bound to deal with at least two of them. It is merely a matter of adding to their next order when the traveller comes round. Push it a bit.

Some foreign terms and names are included in case you buy another curry book in which they are referred to in that way.

* ANCHOVY SAUCE. Keep a bottle of this strong fish

29

sauce to use in curries wherever Blachan, Trassi or Terassi are indicated in a recipe.

ANISEED. Used in some curries, the flavour is so strong that it must be used with care as it is not to everyone's taste.

BLACHAN or *TRASI* or *TERASSI*. A kind of crumbly cake of dried, pounded and rotted shrimps which can be bought at Chinese or Indonesian food shops. Fry it with the other spices before use, or wrap it in a piece of foil and roast it in a frying pan on top of the stove for a moment or two. The foil is to keep the smell under control. Keep spare blachan in a lidded jar. As a substitute use shrimp paste, anchovy paste, or, best of all, anchovy sauce.

BOMBAY DUCK. This is a very smelly kind of dried fish. Cooked in fat or baked in the oven till crisp, it is then crumbled and sprinkled over rice or curry and adds a lot of flavour. But it smells horrible!

CARAWAY. Usually comes as whole seeds, but sometimes ground. It is an important digestive curry spice, with its own very special flavour.

* *CHILLIES*. Green chillies (hari mirchi) are usually used as part of pickles and chutneys or uncooked as a 'sambal' or garnish. They are eye-wateringly hot, and a bit of an acquired taste.

Red chillies (lal mirchee) which are usually used in their dried form (ripe green chillies) or as chilli powder, are very, very hot and must be used with care. Indonesian recipes use them extensively to supply hotness, and many curry recipes include chilli powder. Watch it: most recipes wildly overstate the number (or quantity) of chillis to be used and it is the one ingredient which will completely ruin a dish if it is overdone. We have not had our palates blunted by years of eating the stuff, neither do we live in a climate so hot that we need to be induced to sweat constantly. The recipes in this book all have reduced amounts of chilli included. If the first time you make it, it is not hot enough for you, make a note in the book and add more next time.

* *CARDAMOM (Elaichi)*. A strongly scented spice, with a touch of bitterness. It comes in pods containing half a dozen little seeds. Some recipes use the whole pod, broken open. It can also be bought in powder form and this is best used when the pods and seeds are supposed to be ground into a composite lot of spices. Use the whole pods when they are added directly to the food while cooking.

* *CINNAMON (Dalchini)*. The sweet highly scented bark of a tree. It actually kills bacteria so helps food to keep. It comes in small strips of bark, or in powdered form. If a recipe states '1 inch of bark', it means pieces of flake totalling 1 inch long and about 1/16th thick. Equivalent in powder is about half a teaspoonful.

* *CLOVES*. Strong flavoured little dried buds; if used whole they are a bit chewy and may have to be removed before serving. Powdered cloves can be bought and are most useful.

* *COCONUT*. Buy desiccated coconut or use the flesh of a fresh coconut. Many Indonesian recipes include coconut milk. This can be made by pouring water over desiccated coconut and leaving it to stand for several hours before straining it. Use $\frac{1}{2}$ lb/225g per 1 pint/6dl of boiling water. Or buy a whole fresh coconut, break it open, remove and grate the white flesh and cover it with $\frac{3}{4}$ pint/4$\frac{1}{2}$dl boiling water. Leave it for an hour and then strain and squeeze off the creamy liquid. Repeat the process, but leave to stand for 24 hours before straining and you will have another lot of thinner milk.

    Creamed coconut can be bought in packets and this is very useful indeed as it only has to be mixed with hot water to make instant coconut cream or milk for any purpose.

* *CORIANDER (Dhania)*. One of the most important curry spices – buy it powdered in a fair-sized tin, a small pot won't last any time at all. If you buy the seeds whole and grind them yourself, the spice will be even better, and those same seeds will grow if planted in early summer. The leaves can be used for garnish. Coriander tastes

vaguely of orange peel and honey, but spicier. Quite apart from curries, a teaspoonful adds flavour to all stews and meat dishes.

* CUMIN (Jeera). Another absolutely basic curry spice. From the seeds of a member of the same family as coriander and aniseed, it is digestive and pungent, but should not be used in quite such quantities as coriander, although it is just as important.

CURRY LEAVES. Almost identical with the Indonesian Daun Salam with which they are interchangeable, they can be bought in packets at Indian food shops, otherwise substitute bay leaves.

DAUN SALAM is mentioned frequently in Indonesian recipes. Use bay leaves instead.

FENNEL. Sometimes used in curries, another member of the caraway family.

FENUGREEK. Spicy and slightly bitter seeds used in some recipes. It can also be bought powdered.

* GARAM MASALA can be bought ready-made in tins. It is a mixture of cumin, peppercorns, cloves and cardamom, and should be sprinkled over food, especially vegetables, just before cooking is finished, as it makes a tasty crust.

* GARLIC. Nothing unusual about this herb. Extensively used in curry cookery.

* GINGER. This supplies hotness and flavour. Fresh ginger is fine if you can get it, use it peeled and mashed. Green ginger can be bought ready peeled and spiced in small tins and is often used for kebabs and curry making generally. Dried ginger roots are so hard that they are not much use except to flavour chutneys, having being bruised on the work bench with a hammer! Dried powdered root ginger is extremely useful as a curry spice. Expensive root ginger preserved in syrup keeps for ever and, used in small quantities, is marvellous in curries.

KEMIRI NUTS are also used in Indonesian cookery. Brazil nuts or walnuts are a perfectly good substitute.

* KETJAP is soya bean sauce, see Soy.

LAOS can be bought from Indonesian stores and does impart some flavour, but it is never essential, so don't worry if you cannot get it.

LEMON GRASS (Serai) can be bought in Indian, Chinese and Indonesian shops, either whole or powdered. It is useful but not essential, and a drop or two of lemon juice will substitute almost the same flavour. Or use leaves of the herb Melissa, usually known as Lemon Balm.

* *LIME.* Small sour-tasting citrus fruit like a little lemon. It can be bought in this country and used where specified. Lime juice can now be bought in squeezy packs, and that is fine for all uses. A spoonful or two of Rose's Lime Juice makes a good if sweet substitute.

MACE is not extensively used in curry making. It is rather like nutmeg (from the same plant) but less strong.

* *MUSTARD.* Dry mustard is used in curry recipes to add hotness.

MUSTARD SEEDS. Not especially hot, but nutty in flavour, used in some curries.

* *NUTMEG.* Used in some curries and extensively used in Indian sweets.

* *PEANUTS.* Much used in Indonesian cookery. Use shelled raw peanuts, or crunchy peanut butter (see Sate Sauce), it saves a lot of trouble.

POPPY SEEDS are sometimes used in curries. Toasted poppy seeds have a nutty flavour.

SAFFRON, like turmeric, imparts both yellow colour and flavour; but it is so expensive that it can only be used sparingly, usually in rice. So much would be needed in curries themselves that it would be ruinous.

SANTAN see Coconut.

SESAME SEEDS. Little nutty seeds not used a lot in curry cookery.

* *SOY SAUCE.* This is made from soy beans and is an almost essential ingredient in Indonesian cookery, and very useful in curry cooking generally. It is salty and yet sweet and imparts its own special flavour. Use it sparingly as a sauce or it smothers all other flavours.

TAMARIND. A sour fruit that is an ingredient of many curries, but it is hard to get in this country. Use green apples as a substitute for bulk, or a squeeze of lemon or lime juice for flavour. Or a dessertspoonful each of plum jam and lemon juice well mixed together.

TERASI or *TRASSIE.* The same thing as Blachan (see page 24)

* *TURMERIC (Haldi).* Essential curry ingredient. Astringent yellow spice bought as powder. It imparts flavour and the characteristic yellow colour to curries.

VETSIN or *MONOSODIUM GLUTAMATE.* Readily available and widely used by the Chinese as a taste sharpener, it nevertheless imparts a rather too salty flavour to most foods. It is extensively used in tinned and other processed foods in the West, supposedly to enhance flavour. Many people think that it is destructive to all subtle flavour and is best forgotten.

Chapter 2

CURRY POWDER, CURRY PASTE, BEGINNERS' CURRIES, VINDALOO RECIPES

Curry Powder

Several firms produce ready-made curry powders, and pots or packets of made-up powders may be bought in specialist shops. The beginner should not use the latter until she (or he, and that is the first and last time I am going to waste space by using both words) has some experience, and can then experiment.

The curry powders and other ingredients mentioned in this chapter can all be bought from any good grocer's shop.

Most makers produce a mild curry powder and a hot one. Begin with the mild. The hot powder is usually so hot that it masks all other flavours. A tin of hot powder can be kept for the sole purpose of touching up a curry that is a little too bland, by adding half a teaspoonful at a time. Vencatachellums (Vencat) Madras Curry Powder (Mild) in the blue tin made by Sharwoods is my own choice, but it IS a matter of taste. The same maker's powder in the pink tin is considerably hotter.

Curries are not made by adding curry powder to ready-cooked foods, stews, etc; the spices must be cooked, preferably fried, in ghee, oil or butter (see page 29) to release the tastes properly.

The Easiest Curry of All

½ to 1 lb/225-450 g left-over
    cooked lamb, beef or
    poultry
1 large onion
1 large clove garlic
1 cooking apple
1 medium-sized carrot or
    parsnip, or both, or 1
    small tin carrots

1 oz/25 g chopped dates or
    sultanas or raisins
1 tbspn cooking oil or ghee
1 heaped tbspn mild curry
    powder per ½ lb meat
salt

Chop the onion and garlic coarsely and fry them in the oil in a big deep frying pan until golden, add the diced root vegetables, cook for a few minutes, add the peeled and chopped apple and the dates or sultanas. Cook for 5 minutes, then add the diced meat, and as soon as all is nicely hot, add the curry powder. Turn up the heat and let the whole lot cook together, turning and stirring constantly so that nothing burns, until all is a nice golden brown and the curry begins to smell very pungent. Transfer the lot to a saucepan or casserole and add enough water to cover, and salt to taste, and cook slowly on a low flame or in a low oven for at least 1 hour. The longer the better. Curries are only improved by keeping overnight, so can always be made ahead of eating time.

Serve with plain boiled rice (see page 61), poppadums (see page 69), chutneys (see page 112), and sliced raw bananas sprinkled with desiccated coconut.

Dry Mutton Curry

A curry without gravy, so it should be served with thin dahl to provide some liquid.

1½ lb/675 g lean mutton
1 large onion
4 oz/100 g butter or oil or
   ghee
1 large cooking apple

1 dssrtspn chutney
2 tbspn mild curry powder
1 tbspn raisins
salt

Slice the onion finely and fry it in the fat till golden. Add the curry powder and the apple, and after a few moments cooking, the diced mutton and a little salt and the raisins. This must be cooked in a heavy pan with a tight-fitting lid, over a very low flame, even on an asbestos mat. Stir occasionally to prevent burning, adding a little water from time to time if the meat is sticking to the pan. The dish is ready when the meat is completely tender – about 1½ hours.

Lamb Curry

1-1½ lb/450-675 g shoulder
   or neck of lamb
2 tbspn butter or ghee
1 heaped tbspn plain flour
1½ tbspn mild curry powder
1 pint/6 dl stock made with
   chicken stock cube

1 tbspn mild chutney (any
   will do)
1 banana
1 tbspn raisins or sultanas
1 large apple

Fry the chopped onion in the butter until it is golden, then add the curry powder. While that is cooking for a few moments, cut up the meat and roll it in the flour, then add it to the pan. Cook for a few minutes then add the stock gradually, stirring all the time. Transfer to a heavy saucepan and simmer for 1½ hours (or to a casserole and a slow oven). Don't let the liquid dry right out; add a little more stock if necessary. Ten minutes before serving, stir in the chutney, then add the chopped apple and sliced banana and raisins or sultanas.

Pork in Curry Sauce

1½ lb/675 g belly or shoulder pork, or spare ribs
1 oz/25 g butter or ghee
1 large onion
1 heaped tbspn mild curry powder

1 tbspn plain flour
¾ pint/4½ dl chicken stock made with a stock cube
½ tspn ground black pepper
2 tbspn sultanas

Cut the pork into pieces about 2-inches square, and fry it well in the melted butter. Remove it and fry the chopped onion till it is golden. Pour off surplus fat leaving only about a tablespoonful; add the curry powder and flour, and cook, stirring all the time, for 2 minutes. Add the stock slowly, still stirring, until you have a nice thick creamy sauce. Add the sultanas and pepper and the meat pieces, simmer in a covered saucepan or in a casserole for at least an hour. Do not allow to dry out.

Veal in Curry Sauce

As for Pork in Curry Sauce substituting

1½ lb/675 pie veal *plus*
1 apple
lemon juice

Proceed exactly as in the previous recipe, but add the chopped apple when returning the meat to the sauce, and put in a liberal squirt of lemon juice just before serving.

Pork Tandoori

This is a spicy recipe but contains no very hot ingredients.

4 pork chops or pork spare
   ribs
1 carton natural yoghurt (or
   its equivalent home-made
   see page 144
½ tspn ground ginger
½ tspn paprika

1 clove garlic
4 bay leaves
6 peppercorns
1 tbspn tomato purée
grated lemon peel
½ tspn salt

Mix together the yoghurt and all other ingredients. Prick
the chops all over with a fork, put them in an oven-proof
casserole and cover them with the marinade, making sure
that they are well coated. Leave for at least 6 hours then
remove the bay leaves and peppercorns. Cook in a moderate
oven for at least 1¼ hours, basting occasionally and adding
just a little water if the mixture is too dry. If you have an
electric spit or rotisserie then the pork should be spitted
and cooked very slowly and basted frequently. At the finish
there should be enough sauce to coat the chops but not to
run all over the dish. Serve with saffron rice (see page 63).

Special Pork Tandoori

Very like the previous recipe but with some additions.

4 pork chops
¼ tspn ground ginger
1 dssrtspn paprika
1 clove garlic
1 tbspn tomato purée
salt to taste

1 oz/25 g roasted almonds,
   crumbled
large tin of pineapple cubes
   or rings in syrup
1 tbspn lemon juice

Prick the chops all over and put them in an oven dish.
Make a marinade by mixing the ginger, paprika, crushed

garlic, lemon juice, tomato purée and salt with the syrup from the pineapple and pour it all over the chops, making sure they are well coated. Leave for 6 hours and then cook for 1½ hours in a moderate oven, basting several times. If you have an electric spit or rotisserie, spit the pork and cook it very slowly, basting frequently.

Serve on top of saffron rice or yellow rice (see page 63) into which you have mixed the pineapple cubes or rings cut into pieces. Sprinkle the almonds over the meat.

Beef Kebab Curry

Packets of hard thin wooden skewers, which are very useful for kebabs and for the following dish, can be bought at Indian, Chinese and Indonesian food shops. Of course ordinary barbecue or kebab skewers are perfectly satisfactory.

1 lb/450 g stewing beef	1 chunk of preserved ginger
1 oz/25 g butter	4 shallots, halved
¼ tspn salt	2 tbspn natural yoghurt
1 tbspn ground-up onion	1 tbspn hot curry powder
1 clove garlic, ground	4 skewers

Cut the beef into square pieces; cut the onions into chunks and slice the ginger. Thread these pieces on to four skewers alternating meat, onions and ginger. Heat the butter in a heavy pan and add the garlic, ground onion, curry powder and salt, and cook till it begins to brown; add a little water and the yoghurt to make a sauce. Put the kebabs in a shallow lidded pan and pour the sauce over them, making sure they are thoroughly coated. Simmer over a very low heat for at least 2 hours. Serve with plain rice and a curried vegetable. This dish can be made with pieces of lamb, veal, game or poultry.

Meat Balls in Curry Sauce (Koftah)

One of the basic curry recipes, very easy to make.

1 lb/450 g minced beef
1 lb/450 g onions
3 cloves garlic
1 tbspn chopped parsley
1 egg
oil for deep frying

2 tbspn salt
1 tbspn hot curry powder
1 carton yoghurt or its
    equivalent fresh made
    (see page 144)

Re-mince the meat with half the onions and the garlic and parsley. Mix with the egg and form into small balls, about 1 inch in diameter; squeeze quite hard so that they are well consolidated. Deep fry them for about 3 minutes in very hot oil till nicely browned.

Slice the rest of the onions and fry till golden then add the spices and cook, stirring all the time, for 5 minutes. Add the meat balls and cook for another 15 minutes, making sure that the meat balls do not stick to the pan or break up. Add the yoghurt and a little water or stock and simmer for $\frac{1}{2}$ hour with a lid on. Serve with plain boiled rice and any accompaniments you fancy.

Indonesian Nut Mince

An easy recipe which makes a good supper dish if served with basic curry accompaniments – chapatties, rice, sliced bananas – and it is equally good served with ordinary potatoes and vegetables or noodles.

1 lb/450 g minced beef
1 onion
$\frac{1}{4}$ pint/1$\frac{1}{2}$ dl water
2 oz/50 g crunchy peanut
    butter
1 tbspn creamed coconut

1 oz/25 g whole salted
    peanuts
1 dssrtspn brown sugar
2 tspn mild curry powder
salt and pepper to taste
1 tspn lemon juice

Put the mince into a covered oven dish and break it up with a fork. Cook it in a slow oven for $\frac{3}{4}$ hour. Then pour off the fat and use a tablespoon of it to fry the sliced onion till it is soft. Add the onion to the mince with all the other ingredients except the creamed coconut, and simmer for another $\frac{1}{2}$ hour at least until the meat is tender. A few minutes before serving stir in the creamed coconut till it has dissolved and blended.

Legs of Chicken in Curry Sauce

A recipe which can be adapted for any large chunks of poultry or game.

2 legs chicken	1 tbspn mild curry powder
1 large onion	lemon juice
1 large clove garlic	$\frac{1}{4}$ pint/ $1\frac{1}{2}$ dl chicken stock
1 tbspn tomato purée	made with a cube
1 tbspn cooking oil	

Fry the chopped onions and garlic in the oil, add the curry powder and cook for 5 minutes until it gives off a pungent smell. Add the tomato purée, and thin down with stock until it is a nice rich sauce. Add a squirt of lemon juice. Skin the chicken legs and fry them in butter till golden, then put them in a shallow lidded casserole, pour on the sauce and cook in a low oven till the meat is tender. If you are using precooked chicken legs, then all that is necessary is that they be simmered in the sauce until heated through.

Legs of Rabbit in Curry Sauce

Cook in exactly the same way as the above recipe for chicken legs, but substitute two legs of rabbit.

Serves 2 people

Chinese Curried Chicken

Chinese food needs extra salt to bring out its flavour. Chinese cooks use monosodium glutamate, which is also commonly used by food manufacturers everywhere to bring out flavour. I think it just gives everything the same chemical salty taste, but it does improve the extremely simple recipe which follows.

2 chicken portions, or ½ a
   small chicken
1 large onion
1 tspn cornflour
1 tspn white sugar
½ tspn monosodium
   glutamate

¼ tspn ground black pepper
5 tbspn very mild or Chinese
   curry powder
⅓ pint/2 dl chicken stock
   made with a stock cube

Remove the chicken meat from the bone and cut it into 1-inch pieces. Cut the onion into half rings. Mix the cornflour to a paste with a little water, and add the sugar, pepper and monosodium glutamate.

In a pan with the merest trace of oil or butter, fry together the curry powder and the onion, stirring all the time until it is pungent; don't let it burn. Add the chicken pieces and cook for a couple of minutes, still stirring. Add the stock gradually and bring to the boil. Cover the pan or transfer to a saucepan and simmer for about 15 minutes. Pour a little of the hot gravy into the cornflour paste, stirring all the time, and when the mixture is the consistency of cream return it all to the saucepan; still stirring, bring it back just to boiling point. Serve with rice and other Chinese food.

Serves 2 people

Chicken Kebabs in Sate Sauce

Very easy kebab recipe.

1 lb/450 g raw chicken meat	½ pint/3 dl water
1 tspn vinegar	2 tbspn cooking oil
3 cloves garlic	20 small skewers

Cube the chicken meat into 1-inch pieces. Crush the garlic and mix it with the water and vinegar; pour it over the chicken, and leave to marinate for about an hour.

Drain the chicken and put five or six pieces on each skewer. Draw each skewer through the oil and then barbecue, grill or bake in a hot oven for about 20 minutes till done. Serve with sate sauce (see page 110).

Sweet Chicken Curry

4 chicken joints
2 onions
1 tbspn butter ⎫
1 tbspn oil ⎬ or 2 tbspn ghee
2 tbspn curry powder
½ pint/ 3 dl chicken stock
1 tbspn sweet mango
   chutney

1 tbspn blackcurrant jelly or
   other red jam
1 oz/25 g sultanas
1 eating apple
salt and pepper

Remove the skin and fry the chicken pieces in the mixed hot fats until golden brown, then take the meat from the bones. Cook the onions in the pan with the curry powder till soft then add the stock and bring to the boil. Add the chutney and jam and simmer till the sauce has thickened a little. Put the chicken meat back in the sauce and simmer for about ½ hour then add the sultanas and peeled and chopped apple and cook until the apple begins to soften.

Season and serve with plain boiled rice.

Duck Curry

1 duck	1 large onion
4 oz/100 g fresh or frozen green peas	1 heaped tbspn mild curry powder
1 small tin tomatoes	lemon juice
3 cloves garlic	3 tbspn butter

Chop the onion and garlic and fry it in two tablespoons of butter till soft; add the curry powder and cook for another 5 minutes, stirring all the time, and then add the tomatoes. Joint and skin the duck and cut it into serving pieces. In another pan heat the rest of the butter and cook the pieces of duck in it until golden, turning frequently. Then combine the contents of both pans in an oven-proof dish with a lid and cook in a medium oven till the duck is tender. Add the green peas and cook for another 15 minutes.

Add salt to taste and serve with yellow rice and poppadums. The sesame seed and coconut sprinkler (page 107) goes well with this curry.

Curried Rabbit

Rabbit can be curried using any chicken recipe and is a cheap substitute, although it does have a different flavour. Don't try to pass it off as anything but what it is!

1 rabbit	$\frac{3}{4}$ pint/$4\frac{1}{2}$ dl chicken stock made from a stock cube
2 large onions	
1 clove garlic	2 tspn plain flour
2 bay leaves	2 tbspn cooking oil
1 tbspn curry powder	1 tbspn sultanas or raisins
1 tspn curry paste (see page 55)	1 apple
	2 stalks of celery

Skin and joint the rabbit and brown it all over in the oil. Remove the pieces and cook the chopped onions, garlic and celery until soft, then add the curry powder and flour and continue to cook for a few minutes, stirring all the time. Add the stock slowly, still stirring, until the mixture is a medium thick sauce. Return the rabbit pieces, add the apple, bay leaves and sultanas and simmer until the meat is falling off the bones, a good hour. Be careful not to let the sauce dry out. This is ideally cooked in its last stages in an electric casserole or in a casserole in a very slow oven.

Curried Kidneys

12 lamb's kidneys
1 onion
2 tspn curry powder
½ pint/3 dl stock or water

½ tspn salt
2 tspn plain flour
4 tbspn butter

Dip the kidneys in boiling water, drain and dry; skin and remove the white core. Heat the butter in a saucepan and add the curry powder and flour. Stir and when it half thickens add the liquid gradually, to make a thick sauce. Cook the sliced onions in the rest of the butter till soft, add the kidneys and cook for 2 minutes, then add the sauce and simmer over a low flame for about 20 minutes, until the kidneys are well cooked through and the sauce has reduced to a very thick coating. Serve on chapattis (see page 70) or on plain toast, or with yellow or plain rice.

Curried Fillets of Fish

4 large fillets of fish – coley
   skinned and boned will do
3 tbspn butter
1 small onion

¾ pint/4½ dl chicken stock
   made with a cube
1 tbspn mild curry powder
lemon juice

Heat the butter and cook the chopped onion in it until golden. Remove it, and fry the curry powder till it is dark brown. Return the onion, add the stock, and put the fillets into the mixture. Simmer very gently without disturbing them until the liquid has nearly all gone. The fish should be cooked, but firm. Arrange the fillets on a dish, mix a squirt of lemon into what is left of the sauce and pour it over the fish. Garnish with lemon slices, cucumber.

Fish Curry

½ lb/225 g cooked white fish	1 tspn plain flour
1 small onion	⅓ pint/2 dl milk
1 cooking apple	1 tbspn butter
1 tspn (heaped) mild curry	lemon juice
powder	salt and cayenne pepper

Peel and chop the onion and apple and fry them in the butter till golden; add the curry powder and flour, stirring all the time, and cook for a few moments before gradually adding the milk. Simmer for 15 minutes and then add the flaked fish. Heat again but do not boil. Squeeze in lemon juice to taste, add salt and cayenne pepper, and serve with plain boiled rice; sprinkle grated coconut on top and garnish with lemon, cucumber, sliced banana and/or pineapple.

Serves 1 person

Prawn Curry No. 1

Just substitute ½ pint (or ¼ lb/100 g) of shelled prawns or shrimps for the fish in the last recipe.

Shrimps are used a lot in Indonesian cookery. Tinned or frozen ones are fine but expensive; fresh shrimps take a lot of preparation. Dried shrimps from Chinese shops are excellent and can be used up as and when required.

Prawn Curry No. 2

1 pint (or ½ lb/225 g) of
 shelled prawns
2 cloves garlic
3 onions
2 tbspn butter

1 dessrtspn mild curry
 powder
1 small tin tomatoes
salt and pepper to taste

Crush the garlic and chop the onions and fry them in the
butter till golden; add the curry powder and fry for a few
moments longer until pungent. Add the tomatoes and the
prawns and cook for 15 minutes. Season to taste and serve
with plain boiled rice.

Fried Prawns and Bean Sprouts

4 oz/100 g shelled prawns
4 oz/100 g lean pork or
 bacon
3 cloves garlic
½ lb/225 g bean sprouts
 (see page 67) or a tin

1 tbspn soy sauce
2 tbspn bacon fat, or a
 mixture of butter and oil
black pepper

If using pork, try to cook in bacon fat to improve the
flavour, but if using bacon, then additional butter and oil
mixture will do. Crush the garlic and cook it in the fat
for a few moments, then add the pork or bacon cut into
thin small pieces, and fry until crisp and brown. Add the
prawns and the bean sprouts and continue to cook,
covered, over a low heat until the beans are tender but
still crisp, about 7 minutes should do. Season with soy
sauce and a little black pepper (the prawns will have provided some saltiness).

Serve this as a side dish as it is not a substantial meal
in itself. It goes particularly well with Indonesian food.

Pear, Prawn and Pepper Curry

An excellent and quickly prepared curry.

½ lb/225 g prawns or
    shrimps, fresh, frozen or
    tinned (if tinned don't add
    more salt)
1 green or red pepper
1 onion
1 apple
1 small tin pears (drained)
1 tbspn ground rice

2 tspn mild curry powder
1 pint/6 dl chicken stock
    made from a cube
1 tspn curry paste
1 dssrtspn chutney
1 oz/25 g sultanas
1 tbspn lemon juice
1 tbspn butter

Slice the onion and cook it in the butter till soft; add the diced apple and pepper, and continue cooking over a low flame. Stir in the curry powder and ground rice when the apple begins to soften, and continue to cook for a few minutes more. Then add the stock, stirring gently all the time. Add the rest of the ingredients and simmer for about 20 minutes. Season if necessary. If you cook this dish for too long the fruit and prawns begin to break up. Serve with plain boiled rice.

Curried Scrambled Eggs

A quick curry snack.

6 eggs
1 onion
4 tbspn butter
1 tspn hot curry powder

1 large apple
1 small tin tomatoes, or 4
    tomatoes skinned

Chop the onions and fry them till golden in the butter. Strain off the onions and in the same butter fry the curry powder until it is dark brown. Return the onions with the chopped apple and the tomatoes. Cook until the mixture

49

is a smooth paste, beating it with a mechanical beater or blender if necessary. Beat the eggs and stir them into the sauce; continue stirring until they are set. Serve with plain rice or boiled noodles: they should be just ready if you put them on to boil at the same time as you start the recipe.

Curried Eggs, Hard Boiled

Make the sauce as in the above recipe, and pour it over hot hard-boiled eggs.

Curried Egg and Salad

8 hard-boiled eggs	1 tspn mild or home-made
1 dssrtspn butter	curry powder
1 tbspn salad cream or	¼ tspn salt
mayonnaise	green salad

Halve the eggs and remove the yolks to a basin. Add the curry, butter, salad cream and salt and blend thoroughly. Pipe or spoon the mixture neatly back into the egg white halves, and arrange on a flat plate with green salad.

This recipe makes excellent party snacks, in which case the egg halves may be served on brown bread, thin toast or crispbread, or biscuits.

Aubergine Curry

2 aubergines	½ pint/3 dl thick coconut
1 large onion	milk (see page 31)
1 clove garlic	2 tspn white vinegar
2 tspn curry powder	salt
(preferably Ceylon)	cooking oil

Slice the unpeeled aubergines lengthwise into thin slices and sprinkle them with a little salt. Leave them for an hour, wipe off the bitter brown liquid that will appear, and then fry the slices in oil until they are just brown, but not mushy. Drain. Fry the chopped onion and garlic in the same oil, with more added if necessary, until they are golden. Drain off surplus oil and add the curry powder and cook for a few moments. Add the coconut milk and simmer till the sauce is thick, then add the aubergine slices and simmer for a few minutes before adding the vinegar. Simmer on a very low heat until the sauce is really very thick. The trick is to get the sauce thick without overcooking the aubergines to a mush.

Potato Curry

1 lb/450 g potatoes
2 large onions
2 tbspn butter or oil

1 tbspn mild curry powder
$\frac{1}{2}$ pint/3 dl chicken stock
    made from a cube

Peel and dice the potatoes. Slice the onions and cook in the fat till golden, add the curry powder and cook till pungent, add the diced potatoes and cook for another 5 minutes. Barely cover with stock; simmer till the potatoes are tender and the liquid reduced to a sauce.

Curried Courgettes

6 courgettes
8 shallots
oil or butter
2 tspn mild curry powder

$\frac{1}{3}$ pint/2 dl thick coconut
    milk (see page 31)
salt
lemon juice

Slice the courgettes into $\frac{1}{2}$-inch rounds.

    Cook the shallots peeled but whole in butter or oil; drain and sauté the courgettes in the same oil. Transfer all the vegetables to a saucepan, sprinkle in the curry powder and cook for a few moments before adding the coconut milk. Simmer till the sauce is thick and the vegetables soft but not mushy.

Cauliflower and Lentils

1 small cauliflower
1 small tin pease pudding
  (or $\frac{1}{2}$ lb/225 g yellow
  lentils)
1 onion
1 tspn salt

1 tspn mild curry powder
$\frac{1}{2}$ pint/3 dl medium coconut
  milk (see page 31)
cooking oil or butter
lemon juice

Chop the onion finely and fry it in a tablespoonful of butter till golden. Add all the ingredients except the lemon juice, but including the cauliflower cut into florets, and cook covered over a low flame till the cauliflower is tender. Add the lemon juice and serve. The trick is to make the coconut milk with just enough water to make the sauce into a thin cream. By the time the cauliflower has cooked this will have thickened to a good sauce.

If you are using whole lentils they must be precooked, as they take much longer than the cauliflower to become soft (see page 66).

Curried Courgettes

$\frac{1}{2}$ lb/225 g courgettes
2 green chillies
1 dried red chilli
1 oz/25 g desiccated
  coconut

1 tspn mustard seed
1 carton natural yoghurt
2 curry leaves if available
$\frac{1}{2}$ tspn salt
1 tbspn butter

Cut the courgettes into $\frac{1}{2}$-inch unpeeled pieces and chop the green chillies. Mix with the courgettes and cook in just enough salted water to prevent burning, over a low heat. The water should have evaporated by the time the courgettes are cooked. Add the curry leaves and stand the pan on one side while you mix together the other ingredients. Pour half the mixture over the courgettes and mix together. Then fry the rest of the sauce in the butter for 3 minutes, add to the courgettes and serve very hot.

Courgettes and Onions

$\frac{1}{2}$ lb/225 g courgettes
$\frac{1}{2}$ lb/225 g small onions or
   shallots
2 green chillies
2 tspn mild curry powder

$\frac{1}{3}$ pint/2 dl thin coconut
   milk
pepper and salt
1 tbspn butter

Wash the courgettes and slice them into $\frac{1}{2}$-inch pieces. Remove the seeds and slice the chillies. Halve the onions and sauté all three together in the butter. Put all the ingredients into a saucepan and simmer till the vegetables are tender but not mushy and most of the liquid has been absorbed.

Bean Sprouts and Sesame Seeds

1 tin of bean sprouts or 2
   cups fresh bean sprouts
   (see page 67)
1 tbspn sesame seed
2 spring onions

$1\frac{1}{2}$ tbspn soy sauce
pinch of salt and cayenne
   pepper
1 tspn oil

Put the bean sprouts in a steamer and cook over boiling water for 5 minutes. Tip into a dry saucepan. Add all the other ingredients and shake over a low flame till all the ingredients are well mixed and hot. Serve at once.

Buttered Spinach

The longer spinach is cooked the creamier it becomes, and it makes an extremely good curry accompaniment.

2 lb/1 kg spinach	1 tspn ground ginger
2 oz/50 g butter	1 tbspn water
½ tspn salt	

Wash the spinach and clip away any thick stalks or ribs with a pair of scissors. Put it in a pan with the butter, ginger and salt and a tablespoonful of water, and cook over a high flame for 2 minutes, then turn very low and cook until all moisture has evaporated. Transfer the spinach to a heavy casserole or a slow electric casserole, stir it well and cook at the lowest possible heat for at least 1½ hours: be sure it does not burn. Give it a thorough stir with a fork and serve hot.

It can of course be served without the long slow cook, immediately the liquid has gone, but will not be so creamy.

Curry Soup

Vegetable and chicken soup with just a little curry powder to give it a lift.

1 tspn peanut butter	1 potato
4 tbspn left-over chicken meat	1 large carrot
	1 small onion
2 tbspn butter	¼ lb/100 g green beans
½ tspn hot curry powder	1 bay leaf
½ pint/3 dl chicken stock (if made with a cube omit salt)	½ pint/3 dl medium coconut milk
	salt to taste

Sauté the shredded chicken meat lightly in the butter with the curry powder. Stir in the peanut butter and cook for 2 minutes.

Clean and dice all the vegetables. Put them in a saucepan with the contents of the frying pan, the chicken stock and the bay leaf and simmer, covered, till the vegetables are tender but not mushy. Add the coconut milk and reheat till just boiling. Remove from the heat, adjust seasoning to taste and serve at once.

Apple Curry Soup

People are sometimes wary about cold soup, but the following is gorgeous served before a particularly good curry, or even as a starter for any kind of hot meal.

2 big cooking apples	¼ pint/1½ dl apple juice
2 tspn mild curry powder	(Shloer or Apfelsaft)
2 tbspn butter	½ pint/3 dl thick cream
2 pints/1 good litre chicken	some pieces of preserved
stock	ginger

Cook the curry powder in the butter till dark brown and pungent. Stir in the stock gradually, cooking till smooth. Peel and mince the apples, put them in straight away before they discolour, and cook for about 20 minutes until the apples are soft. Add the apple juice and put the lot through a blender or liquidiser. Chill the plates in which it is to be served; just before serving swirl in a good dollop of cream and sprinkle with chopped ginger.

Curry Paste

Ready made curry paste, or vindaloo paste, is richer than curry powder and really should not be used as a substitute for curry powders. Reserve it for vindaloo recipes, in which the meat is marinated for some time in a mixture of paste and vinegar, soaking up the flavours, which it could not do so well from dry powder. However, there are some simple vindaloo recipes to include in this chapter, and I also find that curry or vindaloo paste is excellent for currying vegetables when you are in a hurry or do not have individual ingredients. Some curry pastes are hotter than others, so check before using.

Curried Parsnips or Carrots

½ lb/225 g diced parsnips or carrots or both
1 tspn curry or vindaloo paste

1 tspn butter
pinch salt

Double up the quantities as required.

Put all the ingredients together in a saucepan with enough water barely to cover the vegetables. Cook fast with the lid on, shaking from time to time, until all the liquid has gone and the vegetables are tender. Be careful not to burn them. This should take about 10 minutes.

Curried Carrot and Parsnip Soup

Use any left-over vegetables from the last recipe, or cook a fresh batch.

equal amounts of prepared vegetables to a total of ½ lb/225 g
2 tspn curry or vindaloo paste

1 tspn butter
1 pint/6 dl beef stock made from a cube
1 small pot of natural yoghurt

Cook the vegetables as in previous recipe with the curry paste. Add the stock and put it all through a blender. Reheat the mixture to boiling, season with salt, and swirl in the yoghurt a moment before serving.

Curried Roast Potatoes

1 lb/450 g potatoes
2 tbspn cooking oil

2 tspn curry or vindaloo
  paste

Peel the potatoes and boil them in water for 5 minutes.
Drain. Mix together the oil and the curry paste and pour
this over the potatoes, shaking gently over a low flame until
the potatoes have absorbed the mixture. This only takes a
few minutes. Transfer the potatoes into a shallow roasting
tin or ovenproof dish and roast uncovered in a hot oven
until cooked and crisp on the outside.

Incidentally I always roast potatoes this way, just omitting
the curry paste. They cook in about ½ hour because they
have already been heated through in the boiling water, and
are not swimming in fat or dripping, so emerge crisper and
less fattening.

Chicken Vindaloo

1 small chicken or 4 chicken
  joints
2 onions
2 green chillies
3 cloves garlic
1 slice green ginger

2 tspn vindaloo or curry
  paste (or as specified on
  jar)
½ pint/3 dl water
1 tspn salt
1 tbspn butter

Skin and joint the chicken. Slice the onions and chop the
garlic, green chillies and ginger and fry in the butter till the
onions are soft but not brown. Mix in the vindaloo paste,
then the water, and pour this sauce over the chicken pieces in
a heavy saucepan. Cover and simmer for about ¾ hour, until
the chicken is tender. Remove the lid and cook rapidly
until the liquid has reduced to a thick sauce, add the salt,
and serve with plain boiled rice.

Vindaloo Egg and Vegetable Curry

An excellent easy curry meal which can be made quickly.

1 large onion
1 clove garlic
3 tomatoes or one small tin
  tomatoes
¼ lb/100 g young carrots
¼ lb/100 g potatoes
¼ lb/100 g green beans
¼ lb/100 g peas

¼ lb/100 g parsnips
and/or any other vegetable
  you like or have available
1 hard-boiled egg per person
1 dssrtspn curry or vindaloo
  paste
3 tbspn cooking oil

Chop the onion and garlic and fry them till golden. Add the tomato, chopped, and the vindaloo paste and cook for 5 minutes more. Dice all the vegetables and add them and stir over the flame till all are coated with oil and paste. Transfer to a deep saucepan or heavy casserole and barely cover with water. Cook over a medium flame or in a medium oven till the vegetables are done but not mushy and the liquid has become a sauce. Hard-boil the eggs, halve and serve with the curry and plain boiled rice.

Vindaloo Cold Haddock

This is a good dish for a party, or as a 'different' salad in hot weather.

½ lb/225 g smoked haddock
  or cod
4 tbspn sultanas
1 cooking apple
3 tbspn chopped walnuts
2 tbspn butter
1 or 2 tbspn plain flour

1 tspn vindaloo or curry
  paste
2 hard-boiled eggs
1 tbspn shrimps
¼ pint/1½ dl milk
any salad

Cook the fish by putting it in a flat pan with a little milk and a knob of butter, and either frying or baking it for a few minutes until it can easily be flaked from the bones and skin.

Put the flaked fish in a bowl with the nuts, chopped apple and sultanas. Reserve the milk.

Melt the butter in a saucepan, stir in the flour and after cooking for a minute, gradually add the milk the fish was cooked in till the sauce is the consistency of thick cream. Add the curry paste. Allow the mixture to cook for a couple of minutes and then add it to the contents of the bowl and stir gently so that everything is coated. Chill thoroughly and serve garnished with hard-boiled eggs, peeled shrimps, lettuce, tomatoes, cucumbers, etc.

Beef Vindaloo

2½ lb / 1 good kilo stewing beef
3 tspn curry or vindaloo paste
6 tbspn vinegar

3 tbspn butter or oil
4 cloves garlic
1 large onion
5 bay leaves

Cut the beef into chunks. Mix together the paste, finely chopped onions and garlic and vinegar and rub this all over the meat. Leave it for 24 hours. Heat the butter and add the meat, marinade and bay leaves. Simmer very slowly until the meat is tender and all the liquid has been absorbed. This is a dry and very tasty curry.

Serves 6 people

Pork Vindaloo

1½ lb / 675 g lean pork (in pieces)
3 onions
3 cloves garlic
4 tbspn vinegar

3 tbspn oil or butter
2-inch piece of green ginger (see page 32)
3 tspn curry or vindaloo paste

Chop two of the onions and the garlic very finely and put them in a bowl with the vindaloo paste and the vinegar; work into a smoothish mixture. Put half of this with the pork pieces, mix thoroughly and leave to marinate for 5 or 6 hours, or longer if possible. Then heat the oil and fry the third onion, sliced into rings, and the finely chopped ginger with the rest of the paste mixture. When the onion is soft, add the meat and bring to the boil with just enough water to cover it. Simmer for $1\frac{1}{2}$ to 2 hours until the pork is tender and almost all the liquid has been absorbed.

Curried Fried Fish

fish and chips from a
  'chippie'
2 tbspn cooking oil

1 dssrtspn curry or vindaloo
  paste

Heat the oil and curry paste together in a frying pan till just smoking, then add the already cooked fish (and chips or any other fried snack) and cook in the hot oil for a few minutes. The food will absorb some of the curried oil and taste most unusual.

Chapter 3

RICE, DAHL, CURRY
BREADS, BATTERS

Rice

Really the only invariable rule is that rice in some form or other is almost always served with, or forms part of, a curry meal. There are several 'foolproof' ways to cook rice so that it is light and fluffy, and not a soggy glutinous mass. I intend to give several of these, and you should be successful with at least one method. Always use long grain, Patna or Basmatti rice, NOT pudding rice.

Remember that rice swells when cooking, and a breakfast cup or mug full may not look much but will produce enough cooked rice for four servings. It is starch that makes rice glutinous, and a lot of this can be washed off before use by putting the rice in a nylon sieve and holding it under the cold tap for a few minutes, until the water which has passed through it runs more or less clear.

Method 1. Three parts fill a saucepan with water and bring it to the boil. Add a teaspoonful of salt and then sprinkle in a big cupful of rice. Keep the heat high so that the rice boils fast for 11 minutes. Check a grain or two by nibbling. The rice should be just cooked through, not hard in the middle. Take off the pan and empty the rice into a colander. Hold the colander under cold running water and a lot more starch will wash out. Shake the rice into a buttered dish and fluff it up with a fork. Place the dish in the middle of a preheated oven with the door just ajar, turn off the heat and leave it for about 8 minutes.

Method 2. Wash ½ lb/225 g of rice as above. Put it in a saucepan with ¾ pint/4½ dl of cold water and a pinch of salt. Bring it to the boil on a high heat, keeping the lid on. Do not stir the rice and do not remove the lid, but turn the heat down and cook slowly till all the water has been absorbed and the rice has softened. Take off the lid but keep the rice over the same low heat until it has dried out – about 20 minutes. Rice cooked this way will be dry but not fluffy.

Method 3. As in Method 2, but with only ½ pint/3 dl of water, until the water has been absorbed. Then put the rice into a steamer or colander and steam it over boiling water in a lidded saucepan till it is cooked right through – about 25 minutes.

Method 4. Exactly the same as Method 2, but however much rice you are cooking, make sure that it is covered with an inch of water to begin with.

To reheat rice, just drop it in boiling water and bring the water back to the boil, before draining the rice and putting it into a very hot dish. Briefly put a clean cloth or napkin over the dish and its contents for a minute or two before serving.

Fried Rice

| ½ lb/225 g rice | 1 pint/6 dl boiling water |
| 1 tspn salt | 4 tbspn butter or cooking oil |

Wash the rice thoroughly and then mix the salt into it until the grains look glazed.

Put it into a saucepan, cover it with the boiling water and simmer for about 20 minutes till the water is absorbed. Heat the butter in a frying pan until it is bubbling (but do not let it burn), and then add the rice. Stirring it with a fork, fry it until it is brown. Transfer to an oven dish and let it dry in a very slow oven for 5 to 10 minutes.

Saffron Rice

½ lb/225 g rice
1 onion
1 tbspn butter

1 pint/6 dl chicken stock
    made with a cube
a big pinch of dried saffron

Wash the rice thoroughly and then melt the butter in a saucepan and stir the rice into it until it is coated. Make up the hot stock, add the saffron to it and pour it into the rice. Give it a good stir and then bring it to the boil, reduce the heat, cover the saucepan and cook till the stock is absorbed and the rice soft, which should be about 20 minutes.

Pilau or Pulao

Spelt any way, this is sweet or savoury rice with or without meat or fish ingredients. The basic recipe is as follows:

½ lb/225 g rice
2 oz/50 g butter
1 large onion
1 clove garlic

1 tspn salt
1 pint/6 dl hot water
¼ lb/100 g green peas, fresh,
    frozen or packet dried

Wash the rice and soak it in cold water for ½ hour. Fry the chopped onions and garlic till golden. Put aside. Add the drained rice, salt and peas to the butter and cook for 5 minutes, stirring all the time, over a low heat, then add the hot water and bring it to the boil. Simmer until the liquid is absorbed and the rice tender. Serve topped with fried onion rings.

To improve on this add:
1 oz/25 g chopped blanched
   almonds

2 oz/50 g raisins, with the
   peas

Yellow Rice

1 lb/450 g rice
½ pint/3 dl thick coconut
  milk (see page 31)

1 level dssrtspn turmeric
2 bay leaves
¼ tspn salt

Wash the rice under running water till it comes off clear.
Put the rice in a saucepan with 1 pint of water and the salt.
Bring to the boil, but do not stir the rice. Cook it over a
medium heat till all the liquid has been absorbed, then add
the other ingredients, mix and continue to cook over a
low heat till the rice is tender.

Peas and Rice

1 pint/6 dl water
1 pint/6 dl chicken stock
  made with a cube
½ lb/225 g rice
1 lb/450 g green peas
2 tbspn butter
1 tbspn oil

2 onions
¼ tspn powdered cloves, or
  4 whole cloves
4 peppercorns
4 whole cardamoms
½ tspn powdered cinnamon

Slice the onions and fry in oil and butter till golden and
soft; add the salt and spices and fry for another 5 minutes.
Wash the rice and add it and the peas to the onions and
fry them until the rice begins to brown, then add the water
and stock and cook over a low flame till the liquid is
absorbed and the rice tender.

Savoury Rice Dumplings

These are very useful in certain curries to add to the bulk.
They may be steamed, or cooked in plain water, or in stock,

or in stock specially flavoured with Indian ingredients. This is Akni (see page 117).

½ lb/225 g rice	1 tspn salt
2 oz/50 g split chick peas	

Wash the rice thoroughly and drain and dry it by putting it in a very low oven until it is crisp. Then break it up in a blender or in a mortar. Wash the chick peas and boil them till they are soft. Drain them and add the crushed rice and the salt and stir together till smooth. When the mixture is cool, make it into balls about the size of a billiard ball. Place them in a cloth and tie it up and cook in boiling stock for 25 minutes. If the dumplings are to be steamed, then just put them in a steamer and cook over boiling water for 30 minutes.

Rice and Lentils (Khichri or Kitcheree)

Capable of several flavour variations, this is a mixture of spiced rice and lentils which goes well with meat curries or can be eaten as a snack with chutneys or hard-boiled eggs.

½ lb/225 g rice	1 tspn turmeric
½ lb/225 g yellow lentils or a	3 cloves
tin of pease pudding	1 tbspn garam masala
1 tspn salt	1 large onion
1 tspn ground coriander	4 tbspn butter
1 tspn ground ginger	

Soak the lentils overnight, barely cover with water and cook them until they are mushy. (If using tinned lentils omit this stage.) Fry the spices in the butter for a couple of minutes then add the chopped onion and cook till soft. Add the rice and cook, stirring continuously, for 5 minutes. Add the cooked lentils. Mix together, transfer to a saucepan and add water to come to 1½ inches above the rice. Simmer without stirring until the water is absorbed and the rice is tender.

Pulses

There are supposed to be sixty varieties of lentils in India. In most British shops there are but two or three. Yellow lentils, sometimes called split peas, are excellent for making Dahl; the only trouble is that they take a lot of cooking before they turn into the rather mushy mixture that we like to eat.

Wash the dried lentils, pick out any discoloured ones and leave the remainder to soak for as long as possible, even overnight, before cooking. This reduces cooking time. Then put them in a saucepan with enough water to cover, and simmer them, stirring frequently, and adding more water if necessary to prevent burning, till they turn into porridge, at which stage they may be used in any recipe in this book which specifies 'pease pudding' or 'dahl'.

It is also possible to buy in delicatessens' the green 'split peas' or lentils which are small olive-greeny brown split lentils. These do not take anything like so long to cook as yellow lentils and do not break down into a complete mush, but retain their split texture. They are not specifically used in Indian cookery, but can be substituted for yellow lentils to make a rather different dahl.

Various other types may be available at delicatessens or Indian food shops. If in doubt about cooking them, simmer them in water until the lentils are soft and the water has evaporated, then add a few slices of onion fried in butter or ghee with a pinch of powdered ginger, and a crushed clove of garlic, and perhaps a pinch of turmeric, coriander and cumin. Stir these together and continue to heat for 5 or 10 minutes to combine the flavours.

Chick peas may also be used in the same way.

The small green Moong or Mung beans which are used to make bean sprouts may also be cooked as above.

Growing Bean Sprouts

This is very easy, and if you really like this vegetable, it is well worth doing. They have many other uses as well as being served with curries, especially with Chinese food. Eat them cooked with almost anything, or raw with salads.

Buy Mung or Moong beans in packets (they are usually sold 1 lb/450 g at a time). They look like tiny dull green peas with a white mark on the side.

Get a big jam jar and put a tablespoonful of beans in it. Cover the jar with a piece of butter muslin held on by a rubber band, and half fill the jar with water. Pour it out immediately and repeat the process twice. Shake the jar so that the beans are spread out and leave it on its side in a warm, but not hot, place. Add water and drain it immediately once a day. After a couple of days little sprouts will appear, and in a week you should have a jar full of sprouts. The seeds increase to ten times their volume. When the sprouts are about an inch long, they can be eaten. Wash them, add a few chopped herbs – parsley and chives – and a little pepper, roll them in melted butter and steam them for 2 minutes. Or let the shoots grow to 1½ to 2 inches, tip them out of the jar into a bowl and wash them under a cold tap, stirring with the fingers. The little green shells will come to the top and can be scooped off. Cook these beans by steaming them for not more than 5 minutes over a saucepan of boiling water, or, if you have not got a steamer, cook them in a covered saucepan with just enough water at the bottom to prevent burning, watching carefully to see that the beans don't stick. Use in any of the recipes on pages 48, 53, 74 or serve sprinkled with a little soy sauce.

Dahl

Dahl is made from lentils and is an excellent accompaniment to curry. Indian restaurants serve it at the consistency of thick soup, but many people prefer it slightly thicker so that it does not run into the other food.

1 small tin pease pudding	1 tspn salt
1 onion	1 tspn dry mustard
1 green pepper	1 tspn ground coriander
1 oz/25 g butter	water
½ tspn ground turmeric	

Cook the finely chopped onions and pepper in butter until soft, then add all the ingredients and enough water to make the mixture just thin enough to stir; simmer for ½ hour.

Dahl 2

A very simple recipe which takes a little longer as it is made with lentils which must be softened.

1 lb/450 g red or yellow lentils	1 onion
	2 cloves garlic
1 tspn salt	2 chillies
1 tspn turmeric	½ pinch cumin seeds

Wash the lentils thoroughly under running water and put them in a saucepan with 2 pints/1 litre of water. Bring it to the boil and add the spices, the chopped onion, 1 clove garlic and the whole chillies. Cook for ½ hour until the lentils have become soft and yellow and the whole is the consistency of thick porridge. Remove the two chillies and serve garnished with the cumin seeds and one clove of garlic sliced and fried together in a little hot oil.

Tomato Dahl

1 small tin pease pudding
5 tomatoes, or a small tin of
   tomatoes
2 tspn mild curry powder
1 onion

1 clove garlic
1 tspn dry mustard
salt and cayenne pepper
water

Skin the tomatoes and chop the onion and garlic, put all the ingredients together in a pan and just cover with water. Simmer till the vegetables are soft. Put the mixture through a blender, return to the pan and simmer it until the consistency is that of thick porridge. Serve very hot, seasoned to taste with salt and cayenne pepper.

Breads, Crisps and Batter Savouries to Eat with Curry

Poppadums or *Pappadums* are commonly eaten with curry, and nowhere will you find a recipe as they are extremely difficult to make at home. You can, however, buy them in tins or packets. There are several makes available, some plain and others with specks of crushed garlic in the bread, which is made of lentil flour. Uncooked poppadums are wafer thin and liable to break, so should be handled with care. When cooked they swell immediately to twice their area, but remain thin and very crisp. They are rather salty, and go well with all curries, either crumbled over the top, or kept on a side plate and eaten piecemeal with the food.

To cook poppadums, heat enough clean cooking oil in a saucepan or deep frying pan to make an inch-deep pool. This should be very hot and just smoking. Drop in the poppadum which will immediately begin to swell, hold it flat and submerged with the back of a fish slice. As soon as the oil has covered it and swelling ceased, it will go golden brown and should be removed and drained on a kitchen towel. The cooking takes about 30 seconds. If the oil is not hot enough the poppadum will not expand. Serve within $\frac{1}{2}$ hour of cooking.

Chapatty flour can be bought from Indian delicatessens

and is best for *Chapattis*. Wholemeal flour may be used, but is much more starchy. It is also used for *Parathas* and *Puris*.

Bessan is very absorbent flour made from chick peas. Gram flour is made from lentils.

Rice flour is used in some recipes and can be bought from Indian grocers.

Ordinary plain white flour is a good substitute in many recipes. NOT self-raising flour. Where a lot of thickening or binding is required, cornflour may be used. It is very fine and very absorbent, so should be used with care or it may make the finished product a little too gluey.

Chapattis

The second most popular form of bread to eat with curries. They do not contain yeast and are very filling, so a little goes a long way.

½ lb/225 g chapatty or wholemeal flour	¼ pint/1½ dl water 1 tspn salt

Put the flour and salt in a basin and add the water, mixing and kneading the stiff dough until it becomes lightly elastic. This will take at least 5 minutes. Put the lump of dough into a piece of greaseproof paper and twist the ends up to close it. Leave it in a warm place for 30 minutes during which time it will rise just a little. Turn it out on to a floured board and roll or shape it lightly with your hands into a long roll. Cut the roll into 12 equal pieces and roll these out until they are paper thin.

Using a griddle or a heavy frying pan, clean but ungreased and VERY hot, cook the rolled-out dough for a minute on each side, then wrap in a clean tea towel, to cool a little before serving.

Chapattis are a substitute for rice. Both together with a curry are too filling.

Parathas, Parrattas

Another form of bread, rather more fattening.

Use exactly the same ingredients as for chapattis and proceed up to the cooking stage. Spread or brush each side of the rolled-out raw dough with melted butter, and then cook them on both sides in a heavy frying pan.

Some cooks use white flour for parathas.

Puris, Poorees 1

The same ingredients again, but more fat for cooking, as puris are deep fried.

Proceed as for chapatties until the cooking stage is reached, then drop each rolled-out pancake of dough into deep oil or butter in a frying pan. Turn it immediately and continue cooking until the pancake puffs up. Drain and serve immediately.

Puris 2

To make puris which will puff up even more, add a pinch of baking powder to the flour.

Puris 3

To make savoury puris add $\frac{1}{4}$ tspn salt and $\frac{1}{2}$ tspn of cumin powder to the flour.

Hong Kong Crisps, or Shrimp Crisps, or Prawn Crackers
These go very well with curries, particularly Indonesian and Chinese types of spiced foods. They can be bought in

packets, and the best are those sold in Chinese or Indonesian food shops which have a definite flavour of shrimps.

To cook, drop a few at a time into VERY hot oil and hold them down with a fish slice for about 2 seconds until they puff up.

Pakora 1

This is vegetables or shrimps or lobster pieces fried in spiced batter, which is best made using bessan, gram or chick pea flour. Failing these use plain flour, although the result will not be quite the same.

6 oz/150 g flour	¼ tspn cayenne pepper
¾ pint/4½ dl water	1 tspn ground coriander
¼ tspn turmeric	1 tspn salt

Sift the flour into the water, stirring all the time until the mixture is the consistency of thick cream, just pourable. When you are sure it is smooth, leave it to stand in a warm place for ½ hour and then beat in the spices. Dip pieces of vegetable or shrimp or lobster into the batter and deep fry in hot oil till golden.

Slices of raw carrot, parsnip, boiled potato or aubergine, courgette, cucumber, green pepper, cauliflower, spinach leaves, celery, can all be used. When using fish, simmer it for a few minutes in a little stock with a clove of garlic crushed into it, before dipping it in the batter and frying it.

Pakora 2

A richer batter for Pakora.

6 oz/150 g flour	½ tspn chilli powder
½ pint/3 dl natural yoghurt	½ tspn dry mustard
¼ lemon	pinch black pepper
1 medium onion	pinch salt

72

Put all the ingredients except the flour into a liquidiser and blend till smooth. Sift the flour into the mixture, whisking all the time, until it is a thick batter which will stand momentarily in peaks when pulled up with a fork.

Dip the vegetables or fish into this and deep fry in very hot oil.

Pakora 3

Plain batter for savouries. It is best made with chick pea flour but plain flour can be used.

2 tbspn plain flour   pinch salt
3 tbspn milk

Mix all together and beat till smooth. Dip whatever is to be cooked into this mixture and fry in medium-hot oil till brown and crisp. Drain on a paper towel and serve with lemon pieces.

Fried Curry Puffs

Excellent for party snacks or for using up leftovers.

½ lb/225 g plain flour   pastry will not have such a
⅓ pint/2 dl thick coconut   good flavour)
   milk (see page 31) or   ½ tspn salt
   ordinary milk (but the

Fillings can be any type of meat, fish or vegetable curry not containing rice.

Mix the flour and salt and make into a soft dough with the coconut milk. Roll out thinly and cut into 4-inch circles. Place a spoonful of filling on each circle, fold over and seal with milk or egg white, crimping the edges together with the fingers. Deep fry in hot oil (preferably peanut) until golden brown. Serve hot or cold.

Spring Rolls

Very much a Chinese recipe, excellent with Chinese and Indonesian curries, or as a snack.

Batter

5 oz/125 g plain flour	¾ pint/4½ dl water
1 oz/25 g cornflour	cooking oil
4 eggs	

Sift the flours together and break into them the eggs, stirring till blended. Add enough water to produce a batter the consistency of thin cream. Put just enough oil in a small frying pan or omelette pan just to moisten the bottom, heat it, and then pour in enough batter to cover the bottom of the pan. Cook over a medium flame and when the pancake has set, lift it out and place it on the back of an upturned plate. Continue until all the batter has been used and you have a pile of pancakes.

Filling

1 tin or ½ lb/225 g bean sprouts	*plus*, to make a special filling 6 water chestnuts
4 oz/100 g fresh, frozen, or tinned prawns or shrimps	4 oz/100 g lean pork or bacon
2 onions	1 small turnip
2 cloves garlic	6 spring onions
1 dssrtspn soy sauce	4 tbspn oil
1 tspn sugar	

Heat the oil and cook the chopped onions and garlic till golden and drain and put aside. Cook the shrimps and pork or bacon in the same fat. Add the chopped spring onions, water chestnuts and grated turnip, cook for a few minutes

74

longer, add enough water to moisten the mixture and simmer them till tender. Add the previously cooked onions and bean sprouts, soy sauce and sugar and stir together. Fill each pancake with this mixture and tuck in the ends. Then cook the rolls in very hot deep oil until crisp, and serve immediately.

Samosas

Described elsewhere in this book as a kind of Indian Cornish Pasty, these are little cones of dough filled with any mixture of seasoned meat and vegetables that you like, including left-over curry, deep fried.

½ lb plain white flour	2 tbspn melted butter
1 tspn salt	2 tbspn natural yoghurt

Work the melted butter into the flour and then add the yoghurt and mix and knead to a stiff dough. Shape into balls and roll out very thin, about 9 inches in diameter. Cut each pancake in half and roll it into a cone. Fill it to the top, turn the flap over and seal it by damping with a little milk and pinching together. Deep fry and serve either hot or cold.

Filling
Mashed potatoes, a few green peas, chopped parsley, mint, onion, cooked minced meat, left-over curry. In fact any tasty mixture.

Chapter 4

CURRY POWDERS AND PASTES MADE FROM GROUND SPICES, INTERMEDIATE CURRY RECIPES

Now for making up your own curry powders from ready ground spices. You can always make up a batch of mild curry powder and then add chilli powder to it to make it hotter. As a general rule, the redder a powder looks the hotter it is, and that is because chillies are red.

Basic Curry Powder

2 tbspn coriander	1 tbspn ginger
2 tbspn turmeric	1 tbspn dry mustard
2 tbspn black pepper	1½ tbspn cardamom
2 tbspn cinnamon	1½ tbspn garlic salt
2 tbspn cumin	1½ tbspn poppy seeds
1 tbspn fenugreek	1½ tbspn chillies

To make this hotter add half a tablespoon each of mustard and chilli.

To make it milder, reduce the amount of chilli.

Omit the cinnamon and cardamom to make a less sweet and scented powder.

Blend well together, sprinkling with a little vinegar, put into an airtight jar where it will keep for ages.

Basic Curry Paste for Meat and for Adding to Other Spices

1 dssrtspn nutmeg
½ tspn ground cloves
½ tspn ground caraway
½ tspn cinnamon
pinch chilli powder

2 tbspn anchovy sauce
1 tspn paprika
enough malt vinegar to
    make a paste

Mix thoroughly and keep in an airtight jar, or the paste will soon go crumbly. These quantities do not make very much paste, but you only need about 2 teaspoonsful per pound of meat, combined with half a pint of liquid. Poultry and fish need only half that quantity of paste and liquid.

Mulligatawny Soup

8 peppercorns
1 bay leaf
1 sprig parsley
1 sprig thyme
rind of ½ a lemon
¼ pint/1½ dl coconut milk
    (see page 31)
1 medium onion
1½ pints/9 dl beef stock
    made with a cube

2 tbspn butter
2 tspn curry powder
1 tspn curry paste
2 tbspn plain flour
¾ pint/4½ dl milk made from
    dried milk powder (less
    likely to curdle)
1 tspn lemon juice
salt and pepper
2 tbspn cooked rice

Put the first five ingredients into a little muslin bag and simmer them in the stock for ½ hour. Remove them. Chop the onion finely and fry it in the butter till pale yellow, stir in the curry powder and paste and the flour, and cook them gently until the flour has blended with the butter. Mix together the flavoured stock and the dried milk and add this, slowly stirring all the time. Add the coconut milk and the lemon juice and season to taste. Simmer for $\frac{1}{2}$ hour and then put it through a liquidiser or a sieve and reheat. Serve with a sprinkling of cooked rice on top.

Easy Chicken Mulligatawny

Boil up the carcass of a roasted chicken and substitute the stock and any chicken pieces to enrich the above recipe. Add salt if no stock cube has been used.

Spiced Vegetable Soup

$\frac{3}{4}$ lb/325 g diced potatoes, parsnips, carrots, cabbage, turnips
$\frac{3}{4}$ pint/4$\frac{1}{2}$ dl thin coconut milk (see page 31)
1 onion
1 clove garlic
1 tbspn cooking oil
2 bay leaves
1 stalk lemon grass or $\frac{1}{2}$ tspn grated lemon rind
$\frac{1}{2}$ tspn turmeric
$\frac{1}{4}$ tspn laos powder or $\frac{1}{2}$ tspn garam masala

Chop the onion and garlic finely and put them in an electric blender with the turmeric, laos or garam masala and the cooking oil, and blend them until they are all quite smooth. Put them into a hot pan and fry gently for a few minutes. Stir in the coconut milk and bring it all to the boil. Add the chopped vegetables, bay leaves and lemon grass and simmer until the vegetables are just tender, but not mushy.

Indonesian Fried Chicken

One of the best curried chicken recipes, this can be made

78

using uncooked chicken portions, or, to save time, with ready-cooked chicken pieces.

4 chicken portions	1 tbspn brown moist sugar
1 dssrtspn coriander	1 onion, chopped
1 tspn cumin	1 clove garlic, chopped
1 tspn turmeric	½ tspn terassi or anchovy
½ tspn laos (not essential)	sauce
¾ pint/4½ dl thick coconut	1 tbspn lemon or lime juice
milk	cooking oil for deep frying
pinch salt	

Put the skinned chicken and all the ingredients except lemon juice into a saucepan, and cook together until the chicken is done and the liquid nearly all absorbed. If the chicken has already been cooked this can be done over a high flame (but do not burn) to evaporate the liquid quickly.

Then fry the chicken pieces in very hot deep oil until they are brown and crisp and drain and serve with any of the sauce which may be left. This curry goes well with vegetables and peanut sauce (see page 110) and plain boiled rice, or saffron rice.

Chicken and Vegetable Curry

This is a little different, but is only for those who enjoy green chillies.

1 chicken, jointed and	2 tbspn green ginger
skinned	2 tbspn butter
3 large onions	1 tbspn cooking oil
3 cloves garlic	a little chilli powder to taste,
1 small tin tomatoes or 4 or	say ¼ tspn (only if you like
5 fresh ones (green	it really hot)
tomatoes will do)	1 tspn salt
4 green chillies	water

Slice and fry the onions and garlic. Add the tomatoes and the ginger, chopped small. When the vegetables are golden, add the chicken pieces, chilli powder and salt and a cupful of water. Simmer, covered, until the chicken is tender. Add the chillies cut lengthwise. Cook for another 5 minutes, and serve with plenty of boiled rice.

Minced Lamb Kebabs

You really need good metal kebab skewers to make these.

1 lb minced lamb	2 tspn garam masala
2 onions	1 tbspn chopped parsley
3 tbspn white breadcrumbs	1 tbspn chopped mint
1 tbspn chopped green pepper	1 tbspn lemon juice
½ tspn salt	1 egg

Mix together the meat, breadcrumbs, spices, green pepper and chopped onion and put the whole lot through the fine blade of a mincer. Add the lemon juice and lightly beaten egg, and make the meat into 2-inch balls. Thread them on skewers and carefully mould them into long shapes on the skewers. Grill them under a low flame, or cook in the oven. When the kebabs slide along the skewers, they are done. Serve them with green salad, cucumber coolers (see page 104) and chapattis (see page 70)

Lamb Kebabs

1 lb/450 g lamb. Use leg or shoulder meat, as lean as possible	2 tbspn natural yoghurt
	1 tspn cayenne pepper
	1 tbspn ground coriander
1 tspn ground ginger	1 tspn salt
1 tspn turmeric	butter
1 tbspn poppy seed	

Cut the lean meat into 1-inch cubes, removing as much fat as possible. Mix all the spices together except the coriander and salt, add the chopped onion and yoghurt, and work it in a blender to make a paste. Prick the meat all over and then cover it completely with the paste and leave it for 1 hour or longer if possible.

Then thread the meat on to skewers and grill it under a medium grill, turning frequently. When the meat dries, baste it with melted butter and continue cooking until it is crisp and brown, basting frequently. Mix together the ground coriander and salt and roll the cooked kebabs on their skewers in this and cook again under the grill until the salt and coriander turns crusty. Serve at once with lemon wedges, green salad and chapattis.

Diced Pork in Coconut Sauce

1 lb/450 g pork, diced
1 tbspn brown sugar
4 brazil nuts or walnuts
1 dssrtspn coriander
1 tspn cumin
½ tspn laos (not essential)
1 piece lemon grass
1 tbspn lemon juice
½ tspn salt

2 onions
2 cloves garlic
½ tspn terassi or anchovy
    sauce
1 pint/6 dl thick coconut
    milk (see page 31)
2 bay leaves
cooking oil

Put the diced pork in a bowl with all the spices and the lemon juice, mix thoroughly and leave to stand for an hour. Chop the onion and garlic and fry them in hot oil until soft, then add the pork and its marinade and the bay leaves and lemon grass and nuts and fry altogether for 5 minutes. Add the coconut milk and simmer in a covered pan until the pork is tender and the sauce has thickened.

Serve with yellow or saffron rice (see page 63) and a curried vegetable.

Sate Steak

Sate dishes are made with meat roasted on spits or skewers over a hot fire and served with spiced peanut sauce. For our purposes the skewered meat may be grilled or cooked in a hot oven or even barbecued, the result is essentially the same. The better the cut of meat used, the tenderer the sate will be, so do not use stewing meat.

1 lb/450 g lean steak, diced
1 clove garlic
1 tbspn soy sauce
2 tbspn lemon juice
1 tbspn brown sugar

1 tbspn cumin
½ tspn grated lemon peel
4 tbspn brandy or sherry
pinch salt

Mix all the ingredients together, pour them over the diced meat and leave it to marinate overnight if possible, or for at least 4 hours.

Skewer the meat and grill or cook it in a hot oven, basting frequently with the marinade until it is all absorbed. Serve with any of the peanut sauces on pages 110–12).

Chicken Sate

This is very easy to do, not requiring such a complicated marinade as the steak. It can be made with raw chicken, but is easier to make with ready-cooked chicken, and will be quicker to do. The meat will be drier, which – especially when the alternative is frozen chicken – is an advantage.

1 chicken, cooked
1 tbspn freshly ground
  black pepper

1 tspn salt
2 tbspn soy sauce
3 tbspn cooking oil

Cut the chicken meat into convenient pieces off the bone, and put it in a paper or polythene bag with the pepper and salt; shake them around till all the meat is well seasoned.

Add a little more pepper and salt if there does not seem to be quite enough.

Skewer the meat and grill or barbecue or roast it, basting very frequently with the mixture of soy sauce and cooking oil. When the meat is nicely browned, serve it on the skewers with any of the peanut sauces on pages 110–12).

Special Sate

To turn either the Steak Sate or Chicken Sate into something a little more complicated, add the following:

12 small pickling onions, or 6 shallots	12 button mushrooms 6 small tomatoes, halved

Boil or steam the onions for a few minutes to be sure they are heated right through, and when skewering the meat, put one piece of onion, one piece of tomato, and one mushroom between each two pieces of meat.

Pork Sate

Pork needs a hotter marinade to bring out its flavour.

1 lb/450 g diced lean pork	2 tbspn soy sauce
$\frac{1}{2}$ tspn chilli powder	1 onion, finely minced
$\frac{1}{2}$ tspn salt	1 clove garlic, finely minced
1 tbspn lemon juice	2 tbspn cooking oil

Mix together all the ingredients thoroughly, coat the pork pieces with them, and leave for at least 2 hours before cooking. Skewer the pork, with mushrooms, tomatoes and small onions as in the Special Sate recipe if required. Cook under a grill or in the oven, basting frequently, till the pork is browned and tender. Serve with any of the peanut sauces on pages 110–12).

Having tried out these sate recipes you will see that it is easy to cook any meat or game this way, either using raw or cooked meat. The trick is a good marinade allowed to soak in thoroughly, a hot grill, barbecue or oven, or of course a rotisserie if you have one, and a good peanut sauce. Plain green salads and plain boiled rice go very well with these dishes.

Spiced Spare Ribs

1 lb/450 g pork spare ribs	4 cloves garlic
1 tbspn coriander powder	1 tbspn anchovy sauce
½ tspn black pepper	1½ tbspn soy sauce

Put the garlic through a garlic press and mix the pressed garlic with the coriander, black pepper, anchovy sauce and soy sauce. Put the spare ribs in this to marinate for at least 1 hour, then grill or barbecue them until tender. This marinade can also be used for rump steak, or for seasoning a roast of beef or pork before cooking.

Sweet and Sour Pork Balls, Indian Style (Chasnidarh)

1 lb/450 g minced pork	2 tbspn brown sugar
1½ pints/9 dl stock	1 tbspn cornflour
2 tspn ground cumin	3 tbspn vinegar
¼ tspn paprika	1 tspn ground ginger
1 tspn fenugreek	2 large onions
¼ tspn black pepper	1½ oz/40 g butter
½ tspn salt	

Mix the minced meat thoroughly with the cumin, fenugreek and paprika and shape into little balls about 1 inch in diameter. Fry these in butter till crisp and brown.

Mix together the sugar and cornflour, salt and vinegar

and simmer until the syrup is thick and transparent. Simmer the meat balls in this syrup for 15 minutes. Slice the onions and fry them in the remaining butter (add more if necessary) with the ground ginger till soft, add them to the pork and sauce. Cook for a further 35 minutes and serve with rice or chapattis.

Savoury rice dumplings (see page 64) may be added to this dish to make more of it.

Burmese Beef Curry

This beef curry does not contain many highly flavoured spices, but is none the less very tasty and easy to make.

2 lb/1 kg lean stewing steak	$\frac{1}{4}$ tspn chilli powder
4 onions	$\frac{1}{2}$ pint/3 dl beef stock
3 cloves garlic	1 tbspn soy sauce
2 tspn turmeric	4 tbspn cooking oil
1 tspn ground ginger	

Chop the onions and garlic and fry them till golden in the oil. Cut the meat into cubes and add it, with the spices; cook until the meat is thoroughly coated. Add the stock and transfer the food to a saucepan. Simmer for $1\frac{1}{2}$ hours till the meat is absolutely tender. Stir in the soy sauce and season with salt to taste. Serve with plain boiled rice and any other accompaniments you fancy. Some curried parsnips (see page 56) go well with this.

Serves 6 people

Beef Curry from Leftovers (Jhal Farzi)

1½ lb/675 g cooked beef
2 onions
2 cloves garlic
1 tspn ground ginger
1 tspn ground coriander
½ tspn ground turmeric
½ tspn chilli powder
½ tspn garam masala
1 tbspn plain flour

2 oz/50 g sultanas
2 tbspn butter
1 tbspn cooking oil
1 pint/6 dl beef stock
¼ pint/1½ dl coconut milk
    (optional) (see page 31)
juice of 1 lemon
1 tbspn plum jam (optional)

Cut the meat into small cubes and roll them in the flour. Brown them in the hot fat and remove them. Chop the onions and garlic finely and cook them in the fat till golden, add the spices and cook for a few minutes till pungent. Put these into a saucepan with the meat and all the other ingredients and simmer gently until the sauce has become thick, which should take about 1 hour. Some people like this dish dry, in which case continue cooking, without burning, until all the liquid is evaporated and the meat is left moist and crusted with the spices.

Serve sprinkled with Bombay Duck if liked, and with plain rice and plenty of side dishes. Dahl (see page 67) goes well with this curry.

Moslem Beef Curry (Kormah)

This is a much more flavoured and scented curry than either of the last two. It should be braised in a casserole in the oven for the best results, but this is not essential.

2 lb / 1 kg good stewing beef	½ tspn ground cloves
4 onions	1¼ pints / 7½ dl beef stock
1 clove garlic	4 oz / 100 g tin pease pudding
1 tspn ground coriander	1 tspn vinegar
1 tspn chilli powder	2 tbspn butter
½ tspn ground cardamom	4 tbspn oil
½ tspn saffron	

Brown the chopped onions and garlic in the oil and remove them from the pan. Dice the meat, brown it and put it with the onions. Fry all the spices in the same oil till pungent. Put all the ingredients except the vinegar in a casserole or oven-proof dish and cook in the oven very slowly for 4 hours, until the meat is really tender and most of the gravy absorbed. Add the vinegar just before serving.

Serves 6 people

Javanese Curried Steak

There are not a lot of scented spices in this curry, but plenty of good flavour. It is one of the few Indonesian recipes that does not contain coconut (santan).

1 lb / 450 g good stewing steak	½ pint / 3 dl beef stock
1 tspn black pepper	1 large onion
1 tspn ground ginger	1 clove garlic
1 tspn chilli powder	2 tbspn soy sauce
1 tspn nutmeg	1 tbspn lemon juice
cooking oil (preferably peanut oil)	2 bay leaves
	¼ tspn salt

In two tablespoonsful of oil, fry the chopped onion and garlic and the spices, salt and lemon juice. When the spices are pungent add the diced meat and fry gently for 5 minutes. Then add the soy sauce, bay leaves and stock and simmer for about 1½ hours until the meat is soft and the liquid has thickened.

Serve with plain boiled rice, and gado gado vegetables (see page 124).

Javanese Meat Balls, Hot

1 lb/450 g minced steak
1 onion
2 cloves garlic
2 red chillies or 1 tspn chilli
   powder
2 eggs
¾ tspn terassi or anchovy
   sauce

1 dssrtspn coriander
1 tspn cumin
1 dssrtspn soy sauce
1 dssrtspn brown sugar
1 tbspn lemon or lime juice
oil for frying

Mix all the ingredients together so that they are thoroughly blended, shape them into 1-inch balls and fry them in deep smoking oil till brown and cooked through. Serve with plain boiled rice and a vegetable curry. These balls are excellent eaten cold with an ordinary salad. They make very good party snacks.

Beef Savouries in Batter

1 lb/450 g minced beef
1 tbspn butter
1 clove garlic
1 medium onion
½ tspn chilli powder
1 tspn garam masala
½ tspn ground ginger, or
   small piece green ginger

1 tbspn chopped mint
2 tomatoes
1 tspn salt
1 tbspn lemon or lime juice
½ tspn turmeric
2 tbspn water
cooking oil for deep frying

Put the meat into a casserole and break it up with a fork. Cook it in a slow oven for $\frac{3}{4}$ hour and then pour off the fat.

In a frying pan cook the chopped onions and garlic and tomatoes with the herbs and spices in the butter until soft and blended. Add the meat and the water and cook over a very low flame till the meat is tender. Add the lemon juice, mix thoroughly and allow the meat to cool. Then shape it into small rissoles and dip each one in batter (see page 69) and fry them in hot deep oil till brown and crisp.

Spiced Steak in Coconut Sauce

1 lb/450 g good steak
2 onions
2 cloves garlic
4 brazil nuts or walnuts
1 dssrtspn ground coriander
$\frac{1}{2}$ tspn cumin
1 tspn turmeric
$\frac{1}{2}$ tspn laos
1 tspn brown sugar
$\frac{1}{2}$ pint/3 dl thick coconut milk (see page 31)

2 bay leaves
2 red chillies or 1 tspn chilli powder
$\frac{1}{2}$-inch green or preserved ginger or 1 tspn ground ginger
1 tbspn lemon or lime juice
salt
cooking oil

The steak must be in slabs about $\frac{1}{2}$ inch thick. Cover it with water, add the laos and boil it gently till it is tender. Keep the stock, and cut the meat into strips. Chop the onions and garlic and fry them in the oil with the crushed nuts, chopped chillies, bay leaves and spices. When the onions are soft and the spices pungent, add the meat strips and the lemon juice and fry for a few minutes longer. Next add the coconut milk, and a good pinch of salt and simmer till the sauce has thickened. Take out the meat and grill it till it is brown and crisp, but not too dry, reheat the sauce and arrange the meat strips on rice or noodles or vermicelli and pour the sauce over the top. Serve with gado gado (see page 124) or any vegetable curry.

Curried Egg Soufflé Omelette

6 eggs	pinch black pepper
½ tspn turmeric	1 tbspn butter
2 spring onions	¼ tspn coriander
1 tbspn parsley	¼ tspn cardamom
1 green chilli	¼ tspn cumin
pinch salt	

Separate the eggs and beat the yolks thoroughly. Whip the whites until they stand up in peaks. Add the spices and the finely chopped onion and chilli to the egg yolks. Fold in the egg whites. Spread the butter all over the inside of a baking dish and spoon in the egg mixture. Cook in a preheated medium oven for 10-15 minutes till the omelette rises and sets on top. Serve immediately.

Serves 3 people

Eggs in Hot Coconut Sauce

This is a good supper dish, or curry party side dish without the rice.

2 tbspn butter	1 onion
6 hard-boiled eggs	2-3 cloves garlic
1-3 red chillies, or 1-2 tspn chilli powder	1 tbspn lemon or lime juice
1 tspn laos (not essential)	1 dssrtspn brown sugar
½ tspn terassi or anchovy sauce	¾ pint/4½ dl thick coconut milk (see page 31)
salt	½ lb/225 g rice

Hard boil the eggs, shell and halve them.

Chop the onions finely and fry them with all the spices in the butter till the onion is soft, then add the coconut milk, brown sugar and lemon juice and cook over a low flame till the sauce is thick. Arrange the eggs on a dish, pour the sauce over them, and serve immediately with rice.

Adjust the amount of chilli and garlic to suit your taste; even with one spoonful of chilli the sauce will be pretty hot, with two teaspoonsful it will be very hot for Western tastes.

Curried Mackerel

1 lb/450 g mackerel
¾ pint/4½ dl thick coconut milk (see page 31)
2 onions
2 cloves garlic
4 brazil nuts
½-inch slice of ginger
½ tspn turmeric

2 red chillies or 1 tspn chilli powder
2 slices of lemon
4 basil leaves or ¼ tspn dried basil
salt
4 tbspn tamarind water (see page 33)

Clean the mackerel, then cut down the length of the fish and remove the backbone and as many of the other bones as possible. Cut each fillet into two. Slice the onions finely and cut the chillies in half lengthwise (removing the seeds if you want to make them less hot). Pound the garlic, nuts, ginger and turmeric as finely as possible, then add the onions and chillies and sprinkle in the basil. Boil this for about ½ hour until it has reduced by about a third. Put in the fish and lemon slices, and cook it very slowly indeed for about 10 minutes, stirring all the time to stop curdling. Add the tamarind water and salt just before serving.

Herrings in Hot Sweet and Sour Sauce

4 herrings
4 spring onions
1 clove garlic
½ tspn chilli powder
1 tspn ground ginger
1-3 tbspn brown sugar

1-3 tbspn white vinegar
4 tbspn water
2 tspn cornflour
a few drops of anchovy sauce
cooking oil

Cut the heads off the herrings and scale and clean them. Slash each one a couple of times on either side of the body. Rub in a little cornflour all over them. Deep fry the herrings until they are brown and crisp. In a tablespoonful of oil fry the chopped garlic, ginger and chilli powders for a few minutes, then add the anchovy paste, sugar, vinegar and water, and chopped spring onions. The amount of vinegar and sugar will alter the strength of the sweet/sour taste, but do keep the quantities of each the same. Stir in the rest of the cornflour and let the sauce thicken. Cook for another 5 minutes, then pour the sauce over the hot herrings, and serve with plain boiled rice.

Kedgeree

This name covers a multitude of recipes, but what we know as kedgeree is a gently spiced concoction of yellow smoked fish and rice. The following recipe makes an extremely good breakfast or supper dish.

1 lb/450 g smoked haddock or cod	½ tspn mild curry powder
6 tbspn butter	1 tbspn lemon juice
1 large onion	1 bay leaf
¼ tspn cayenne pepper	salt and pepper
¼ tspn black pepper	¾ pint/4½ dl water
¼ tspn turmeric	6 oz/150 g rice
	4 hardboiled eggs

Heat the butter and fry the sliced onion till it is soft and golden. Add the spices and fry them for a couple of minutes. Add the lemon juice and water, bay leaf, salt and rice, and allow to simmer till the rice begins to soften, about 15 minutes. Add the flaked fish and go on simmering till the mixture is almost dry and the rice cooked. Do not stir more than necessary but take care that the rice does not stick to the pan. You may prefer to transfer the rice to a covered oven dish when adding the fish and to finish cooking in a medium oven till the rice is done.

Serve with halved hard-boiled eggs, and sweet mango chutney.

Fried Fish in Coconut Sauce

2 lb/1 kg fish fillets, sea bream, coley, haddock or cod
1 tspn coriander
½ tspn laos
½ tspn five spice powder
1 tspn terassi or anchovy sauce

2 red chillies, or 1 tspn chilli powder
1 onion, chopped
2 cloves garlic, chopped
4 brazil nuts or walnuts
1 pint/6 dl thick coconut milk (see page 31)
½ tspn salt

Wash the fish and skin it and dry with a cloth. Rub it with salt and fry it in hot oil until brown and nearly cooked. Fry all the other ingredients except the coconut milk together till the onions are soft, add the coconut milk and cook for about 10 minutes. Then add the fish fillets and simmer until the fish is done and the sauce has thickened. Serve it very hot.

Spitted Herbed Prawns

This recipe makes a dish by itself, although not as filling as many other curries. Or it makes an excellent second curry dish for a curry party.

1 lb/450 g shelled prawns
1 tbspn butter
1 tbspn cooking oil
½ tspn dried basil or 2 fresh basil leaves
2 cloves garlic
1 tspn paprika

pinch of cayenne or chilli powder
1 tspn ground black pepper
1 tbspn chopped fresh mint
pinch salt
2 tbspn tarragon vinegar
2 tspn turmeric

Melt the butter and add it to the spices and finely chopped herbs and garlic, and oil, and pour it over the prawns, making sure they are thoroughly coated with the mixture. Leave them for at least 8 hours in the fridge to absorb the marinade. Thread the prawns on to kebab skewers (the fine wooden ones from a Chinese store). Put them in the pan of your grill and pour half the marinade over them; cook under a low to medium grill. When the marinade has dried up add the rest, and turn up the heat and continue to cook rather faster until the prawns begin to darken; turn the skewers over, cook the other side and serve immediately. If you overcook them, the prawns will just shrivel up and go leathery.

Prawns and Peas with Rice

½ lb/225 g rice
1 pint or ½ lb/225 g shelled prawns
2 large onions
½ lb/225 g fresh, frozen or dried green peas, ready to cook
2 tbspn butter
1 tbspn cooking oil

1 pint/6 dl coconut milk (see page 31)
1 tspn chilli powder
½ tspn ground turmeric
¼ tspn ground cloves
¼ tspn cinnamon
¼ tspn cardamom
1 tspn salt
hard-boiled eggs if required

Wash the rice thoroughly under running water and leave it to soak for an hour. Drain it. Chop the onions finely and cook them in the fat till golden; add the peas and prawns and cook them for a few minutes. Add the rice and fry till it begins to brown. Add the coconut milk and all the spices and simmer, covered, over a low flame until the liquid has been absorbed and the rice tender. Serve with halved hard-boiled eggs to make a good supper dish, or without the eggs as an accompaniment to other curries.

Curried Liver for Two

½ lb/225 g lamb's liver   ½ tspn ground ginger
1 onion   ½ tspn salt
1 clove garlic   ¼ tspn chilli powder
½ tspn turmeric   cooking oil
½ tspn black pepper

Slice the onion and garlic and fry them in the oil till soft. Wash and dry the liver and cut it into thin slices. Make all the spices into a paste with a little water and rub this well into the liver slices. Leave these slices to marinate for ½ hour and then add them to the onions in the pan and cook, covered, so that no juices are lost, until the liver is tender. Or place the meat and onions and any sauce into an oven-proof dish with a lid and braise in a medium oven until the liver is done. This way it will be slightly drier. Serve with curried sauté potatoes (see page 96), or freshly made chapattis (see page 70), or mixed vegetables cooked in coconut milk (see page 31).

Spiced Fried Aubergines and Peppers (Bhugia)

Cooked without water, this makes an excellent vegetable accompaniment to any curry. I buy slightly damaged aubergines and peppers cheaply for this dish. One need not be slavish about quantities.

1 large onion   1 tspn garam masala
½ lb/225 g aubergines   1 tspn paprika
½ lb/225 g green peppers   1 tspn salt
1 small green chilli   2 tbspn butter
2 tbspn tomato purée   1 tbspn cooking oil

Cook the chopped onion in hot oil. Cut the aubergines into dice, remove the seeds from the pepper and chop it and the chilli and add them with the aubergines to the onions. Cook until the vegetables are soft, adding more oil or butter if necessary. Add the salt and spices, stir and cook with a lid on for a few minutes more, but do not allow the mixture to burn. Stir in the tomato purée, reheat and serve. Sprinkle just a little more garam masala over the vegetables in the dish if liked.

Sauteed Aubergines, Indonesian Style

2 aubergines
3 onions
1 clove garlic
black pepper
1 tbspn soy sauce

½ pint/3 dl chicken stock
   made from a cube
nutmeg
1 clove
cooking oil

Peel the aubergines and slice them into ¾-inch slices, and sprinkle them well with black pepper. Fry them in oil until they are half cooked and browning slightly. Slice half the onion, and add this with the chopped garlic, clove and a pinch of nutmeg (and salt if stock cubes are NOT being used) and cook for a few minutes till the aubergines slices are coated with this mixture. Add the soy sauce and the stock, cover and turn down the heat and simmer until the aubergine slices are soft but not mushy. Fry the rest of the onions and sprinkle them over the top of the aubergines before serving.

Curried Sauté Potatoes

This can be made with leftover potatoes or with potatoes specially boiled for this purpose.

1 lb/450 g potatoes
1 large onion
3 bay leaves
1 strip of Bombay Duck

1 tspn chilli powder
cooking oil or good dripping
½ tspn salt

Scrub the potatoes and boil them gently in their jackets till just done but not broken. When they are cool enough to handle, strip off the skins and cut them into ½-inch slices. Sprinkle them with half the chilli powder and the salt.

Slice the onion and sprinkle it with the rest of the chilli powder and salt and fry in a tablespoonful of hot oil or fat with the bay leaves, until soft and golden. Add the potatoes and fry together until the potatoes are brown, turning occasionally with a fish slice.

Meanwhile cook the piece of Bombay duck in the oven or under a grill till crisp (see page 108). Just before serving, crumble the Bombay duck and sprinkle it over the potatoes.

If made with leftover potatoes this can be done very quickly. It is excellent served with any ordinary fried steak or fish, or sausage, or as a vegetable with a meat curry. With a couple of fried eggs and some bacon, it makes an excellent snack.

Curried Potato Savoury

6 medium-sized potatoes	1 egg
½ tspn chilli powder	¼ tspn salt
1 tspn turmeric	2 tbspn butter
½ tspn coriander	1 tbspn cooking oil

Scrub the potatoes and boil them in their jackets till done but not mushy. Drain and remove the skins carefully. Cut them into thirds. Beat all the other ingredients (except the oil) until thick. Dip the potato pieces into this mixture and coat them well, then fry in the very hot oil. They are excellent by themselves, or with cold meat or chicken.

Curried Potato Cakes

cold mashed potato
cooked peas
1 green chilli per $\frac{1}{2}$ lb/225 g
  of potato
$\frac{1}{4}$ tspn ground ginger
$\frac{1}{4}$ tspn coriander
$\frac{1}{4}$ tspn garam masala
$\frac{1}{4}$ tspn salt
1 egg
1 tbspn butter
1 tbspn frying oil

Mix all the ingredients together except the egg, and beat that in a separate bowl. Form the potato into flat but solid cakes, dip in the egg and fry.

Cauliflower in Curry Batter

See also 'pakora' page 72.

1 small cauliflower
2 tbspn plain flour or chick
  pea flour
3 tbspn milk
pinch salt
4 tbspn cooking oil
1 tspn curry or vindaloo
  paste

Cook the cauliflower gently till just tender, preferably by steaming it, having broken it down into small florets.

Mix the flour, salt and milk to a thickish batter, and dip each floret in it.

In a small frying pan heat the oil and the curry paste till just smoking and cook the battered florets in this a few at a time till crisp and golden. Drain on kitchen paper and serve hot.

Shredded Fried Vegetables

Known to the Indonesians and Chinese as 'stir fried' vegetables, they must be served crisp and not soggy.

½ lb/225 g vegetables, cabbage, marrow, green beans, young peas in the pod, courgettes
1 clove garlic
1 onion
1 fresh chilli
2 curry leaves (optional)

1 tspn laos (optional)
1 stem lemon grass
salt to taste
2 tspn soy sauce
3 tbspn cooking oil, preferably coconut or peanut oil

Shred the vegetables finely, and chop the lemon grass. Cook all the ingredients except the soy and salt together in the oil in a frying pan, stirring constantly till the vegetables are just cooked but still crisp and crunchy. Add the soy sauce and a little salt to taste and serve at once.

Curried Ladies' Fingers (Okra)

This peculiarly Indian vegetable can be bought fresh in this country now, and all delicatessens sell it tinned. The tinned variety does not have the same flavour as fresh okra, and both can be a little slimy in texture. In this recipe the vegetable is served in a thick onion and tomato sauce.

1 lb/450 g fresh okra
2 onions
3 cloves garlic
1 small tin tomatoes
2 tspn coriander

½ tspn turmeric
1 tspn garam masala
salt and pepper to taste
2 sprigs of fresh mint
butter

Slice one onion and fry it in a tablespoonful of butter till soft. Chop the other onion and the garlic very finely and put them through a blender with the spices, except the

99

garam masala, and a pinch of pepper and salt. Add this mixture to the cooked onions and fry for a few minutes. Wash and top and tail the okra carefully and chop it into ½-inch chunks and add them to the mixture in the frying pan. Cook for a few moments to cover the okra with the spices, then transfer everything to a saucepan and cook over a very low flame, covered, until the vegetables are tender but not mushy. Then add the tomatoes and the garam masala and cook for a further 10 minutes, slowly, to reduce the liquid. Serve hot, sprinkled all over with chopped mint.

Curried Green Beans

½ lb/225 g runner or French beans
salt
4 shallots
2 tbspn butter

1 dssrtspn chopped green or preserved ginger, or ½ tspn ground ginger
½ tspn ground turmeric
2 cloves garlic
1 or 2 green chillies
1 tbspn desiccated coconut

String the beans and chop them into pieces. Cook them in a saucepan with a little water and salt and two of the shallots chopped finely. When soft, remove from the heat and drain off any remaining water (there should only be a drop or two). Chop the other two shallots and the garlic and soften them in butter. Add the ginger, turmeric, cooked beans and chopped chillies and stir together. Cook them for a few minutes longer to blend in the spices, add the coconut, stir once more over the heat and serve hot. The type of ginger used will alter the dish a little, but this makes a good vegetable to serve with meat curries.

Mixed Vegetables Cooked in Coconut Milk (Sajur)

This is a kind of vegetable stew enlivened by the green chillies. It can be made without them but won't have the same flavour.

1 large aubergine
½ lb/225 g French or runner
  beans
1 small tight cabbage
1 small cauliflower
1 large potato
1 large onion
2 cloves garlic
2 green chillies
2 pints/1 litre stock made
  from a chicken stock
  cube

½ pint/3 dl thick coconut
  milk (see page 31)
1 tbspn lemon or lime juice
½ tspn terassi or anchovy
  sauce
1 dssrtspn brown sugar
2 bay leaves
1 tspn ground coriander
½ tspn ground cumin
¼ tspn laos (not essential)
cooking oil

Fry together the onions, chillies and garlic chopped small with all the spices and sugar. Put the diced aubergine, the chopped beans and potato, and the cauliflower broken into small florets, in a saucepan with the stock and cook until just tender. Add the cabbage, shredded, and the fried onions and garlic and the spices. Cook for 5 minutes then add the coconut milk and simmer very gently till all the vegetables are nicely cooked but not mushy. Add the lemon juice, stir and serve.

Steamed Vegetables with Peanut Sauce (Petjel)

1 small cabbage, sliced
1 small cauliflower broken
  into small florets
½ lb/225 g French or runner
  beans

½ lb/225 g bean sprouts
½ lb/225 g boiled new
  potatoes

Steam the green vegetables separately till crisp but not mushy, about 10 minutes, and then make a bed of the sliced potatoes on a dish and layer the vegetables on top.

Pour peanut sauce No 3 (see page 111) all over or serve in a separate jug. Be sure the vegetables and the sauce are good and hot: this is unpleasant when only lukewarm.

Chapter 5

CURRY ACCOMPANIMENTS, SAUCES, CHUTNEYS, PICKLES, STOCK

However simple the curry it is always improved by being served with good accompaniments. These may be extremely simple, or in themselves quite complicated.

Quick Side Dishes

Perhaps the easiest of all, and one which goes with every curry, is sliced *banana*. If you prepare it beforehand, sprinkle it with lemon or lime juice to prevent it from going brown, and this juice in itself improves the taste of the banana.

A sprinkling of *desiccated coconut* on the banana is fine, but there are those who cannot bear coconut. In that case serve a small dish of desiccated coconut separately.

Peanuts fresh or roasted and salted also go well with curries and can be served in a separate dish.

As described in Chapter 3, there are various breads which are served with curries, and *poppadums* should be served with every curry except when *chapattis* or *puris* take their place. When the latter are served, there is no need for rice.

Various raw vegetables and fruits go extremely well with curry. *Green* or *red peppers* sliced and dressed with a little olive oil make a colourful and tasty side dish. Any type of *onion* including *shallots, spring onions* or *pickling onions*, sliced thinly and with just a drop or two of vinegar if liked, may be served by themselves or mixed with sliced *tomato*. Again tomato is fine by itself with just a sprinkling of chopped mint and a little vinegar.

Sliced *cucumber*, served with a covering of natural yoghurt is very cooling with a hot curry.

Sweet apples go well with many curries and can be served cut into pieces or cored and sliced. Retain the skin if it is bright and clean. Mix together 1 tablespoonful of olive oil and one of lime juice and coat the apples with this as it will lift the flavour and prevent them from going brown.

Cucumber Cooler

¼ cucumber
1 tbspn natural yoghurt
1 tbspn top of the milk
¼ tspn salt

¼ tspn dill seeds
¼ tspn castor sugar
1 dssrtspn lemon or lime
   juice

Slice the cucumber very thinly. Mix together all the other ingredients and pour them over the cucumber, coating each slice thoroughly. This should be made immediately before use as the salt will draw water from the cucumber and make the sauce very runny if it is left to stand for more than a few minutes. If you wish to make this accompaniment ahead of time, then put the sliced cucumber in a colander with a good sprinkling of salt and leave it to stand under a small plate with a weight (a bag of sugar will do) on it for about an hour. Then wipe the cucumber dry and continue as above, but omit the salt from the sauce mixture.

Green Sambal

Made from fresh fruit and vegetables, this retains its colour and texture and is delicious.

2 large green apples	½ green pepper
1 small onion or 2 tbspn spring onion	2 tbspn lemon or lime juice add ½ green chilli if liked

Peel, core and chop the apples and place them in a bowl of salted water (1 oz/25 g salt to 1½ pints/9 dl water). After 10 minutes drain and dry them, and mix with the other ingredients, which should be chopped. Sprinkle with the lemon or lime juice and serve immediately.

To make this curry accompaniment the ingredients should be chopped fairly small so that a tablespoonful served on a plate will contain a good mixture of the ingredients.

Onion and Pepper

Another fresh-looking side dish with a strong taste.

1 bunch of spring onions	2 tbspn lime or lemon juice
1 large clove of garlic	salt
1 green pepper	

Chop the onions and pepper quite small. Crush the garlic and mix it with the other vegetables, sprinkle with the juice and a little salt to bring out the taste.

Fresh Carrot Relish

¼ lb/100 g carrots	½ tspn salt
1 small onion or shallot	1 tbspn lime or lemon juice
1 tbspn parsley	pinch caraway seeds
1 tbspn chopped green ginger	

Grate the carrots, chop the onion finely and mix them with the chopped parsley and ginger. Add the salt and lime juice to taste, and leave for $\frac{1}{2}$ hour before serving. A few caraway seeds added to this make an extra flavour.

Yoghurt Relish (Raeta)

1 carton natural yoghurt, or
   home made (see page
   144)
pinch salt
pinch pepper

$\frac{1}{2}$ green chilli
1 sliced tomato
1 tbspn diced cucumber
1 clove garlic
2 spring onions, chopped

Beat the yoghurt with the salt and pepper and then mix in the diced vegetables. Chill for several hours and serve as a curry accompaniment. The quantities of vegetables can be varied and others substituted.

Hot Coconut Relish

This uncooked relish goes extremely well with Indonesian curries, as it contains both coconut and chillies which are staples in that part of the world.

1 long red chilli
2 tbspn desiccated coconut

1 tspn anchovy sauce
$\frac{1}{2}$ tspn salt

Crush the chilli in a mortar or blender, add the other ingredients and mix to a paste, and eat just small amounts as a sauce with any curry.

Sesame Seed and Coconut Sprinkler

2 oz/50 g sesame seed
3 oz/75 g grated or
  desiccated coconut
2 tbspn grated orange rind

2 tbspn lime or lemon juice
pinch ground saffron
¼ tspn cayenne pepper

Mix all the ingredients together, having pounded the sesame and coconut in a mortar or given them a twirl in a blender. Put them in an ovenproof dish and heat in a medium oven for no more than 5 minutes, they must not cook or brown. Remove them and chill, and serve in a dish to sprinkle over food.

To serve as a relish mix with enough natural yoghurt to make a thick paste.

Shrimp and Lentil (Split Pea) Savouries

Excellent for party snacks or curry accompaniments.

½ lb/225 g yellow lentils or
  split peas
2 onions
2 green chillies
slice of green ginger
oil for deep frying

1 tspn salt
½ tspn turmeric
¼ tspn cumin
¼ tspn coriander
a few shrimps or prawns

Soak the lentils in water overnight or for at least 6 hours and then grind them in a blender to make meal. Chop the onions, chillies and ginger and mix with the meal together with the spices and salt. Make the mixture into little balls and then flatten each one on a lightly oiled surface, using a palette knife or fish slice. Press a couple of peeled shrimps or prawns well into the dough, then deep fry each one in very hot fat till crisp.

Spiced Chilli Paste

This is an extremely hot sambal usually served with Indonesian food. For those who like a touch of fire it is easy to make.

5 large red chillies
¼ tspn terassi or anchovy
   sauce
½ tspn brown moist sugar
   (dark)

1 medium onion
1 clove garlic
1 tspn grated lemon peel
pinch salt
oil

Crush the chillies, onions and garlic and fry all the ingredients together in a little hot oil, enough to make a paste. Cook until the mixture is oily but not brown, and stir all the time as the sugar may burn. Serve in a small dish with a non-metal spoon.

Bombay Duck

Buy this smelly dried fish in packets. Cook it by baking it dry and uncovered in a medium oven till crisp. This does not take very long and it is wise to check it every few minutes to see if the fish has begun to brown and curl at the edges, a sign that it is nearly done. When crisp it can be crumbled over curry or used as an ingredient in some recipes.

Aubergines in Yoghurt

A cold vegetable side dish, made piquant with yoghurt and chilli powder, which goes well with almost any curry.

1 aubergine
3 tbspn butter
¼ tspn chilli powder
1 small clove garlic (if liked)

1 small carton natural
   yoghurt, or home made
   (see page 144)

108

Skin the aubergine and dice it. Fry these pieces in the butter with the crushed garlic until soft and golden, but not brown and mushy. Mix the yoghurt with the chilli powder and pour this over the aubergines in a small dish, chill and serve.

Hot Tomato Relish

Serve this as a side dish for those who really like hot accompaniments, and embellish it according to the three recipes which follow.

4 red chillies, or 2 tspn chilli powder
5 tomatoes skinned and sliced, or 1 large tin
1 tspn laos powder
½ tspn terassi or anchovy sauce
½ pint thick coconut milk (see page 31)

2 bay leaves
2 onions
1 clove garlic
1 tbspn brown sugar
1 tbspn lemon or lime juice
salt to taste
cooking oil

Fry together the chopped onions, garlic and chillies with the laos, terassi, brown sugar and salt until the onions are soft, then add the tomatoes and continue frying until the liquid has been reduced (if using tinned tomatoes). Add the lemon juice and coconut milk and the bay leaves and simmer until the mixture has reduced to a thick sauce. Put it through a blender, or if you like it a little chunky, give it a good twirl with an egg whisk, and serve it hot.

Hot Tomato Relish with Shrimps

To improve on the previous relish, fry up to 4 oz/100 g of shrimps in butter and add them to the finished sauce.

Hot Tomato and Shrimp Relish with Eggs

To improve still further, hard boil enough eggs to provide one half for each serving; shell, place in a dish and pour the hot relish over them.

Hot Soy Sauce

To make a hot piquant sauce out of ordinary soy sauce, which can be used with any chicken or fish or rice dish, use the following recipe.

¼ pint/1½ dl soy sauce
1 clove garlic
1 tspn black treacle

½ to 1 (according to taste) tspn chilli powder

Combine all the ingredients in a blender, and serve as a relish.

Peanut Sauce

Peanut Sauce in various forms is used extensively, especially in Indonesian cookery, when it is usually called *Sate* or *Satay* sauce. It is poured over meat or poultry threaded on sate sticks or skewers, or over eggs, rice and vegetable dishes. Very rich and satisfying, it is extremely easy to make, but like all other curry dishes, can be as simple or complicated as you like to make it. In progression here are some recipes, numbered for cross referencing from other recipes in the book.

Peanut Sauce 1

¼ lb/100 g crunchy peanut butter
1 tbspn curry paste or powder

½ tspn chilli powder
1 crushed clove of garlic
water

Mix all the ingredients together in a saucepan and add water until it is the consistency of thick cream. Serve hot. This sauce is fairly hot, but the chilli powder can be reduced if you like it bland.

Peanut Sauce 2

2 cloves garlic
1 red chilli
½ chicken stock cube

¼ pint boiling water
lemon juice
¼ lb/100 g peanut butter

Chop the garlic and chilli very finely and mix them with the other ingredients, heat and cook until the sauce is blended and smooth.

Peanut Sauce 3

1 red chilli
¼ lb/100 g peanut butter
1 tspn brown sugar

1 tspn soy sauce
1 tspn lemon juice

Mix all together in a saucepan, heat and add boiling water, stirring well until it is the consistency of thick cream.

Peanut Sauce 4

1 small onion
4 macadamia nuts or brazil
    nuts or walnuts
½ tspn ground chilli
4 oz/100 g crunchy peanut
    butter
1 tbspn coconut or peanut
    oil

1 tbspn lime or lemon juice
1 tbspn soy sauce
1 tbspn dark brown moist
    sugar, or 1 dssrtspn black
    treacle
salt
⅓ pint/2 dl thin coconut milk
    (see page 31)

111

Mix all the ingredients, except the coconut milk, together in a blender. Then put them in a saucepan with the coconut milk and cook till it is of a thick pouring consistency. Dilute with a little water if necessary.

Peanut Sauce 5

1 tspn ground coriander
½ tspn ground fennel seeds
1 tspn ground cumin
½ tspn ground chilli
1 tspn brown sugar
1 tbspn vinegar
1 tspn blachan, or terassi or anchovy sauce
2 onions

1 clove garlic
4 oz/100 g crunchy peanut butter
⅓ pint/2 dl thick coconut milk (see page 31)
juice of a lemon
2 tbspn peanut or ordinary cooking oil

Mince the onions and garlic and fry them together with all the ground spices and the blachan in the oil until pungent, add the rest of the ingredients except the lemon juice and salt, and simmer for 15 minutes to thicken. Add the lemon juice and salt to taste just before serving.

So here you have five good recipes. If you wish to use fresh peanuts, shell them and dry fry them until brown, then crush them in a mortar or in a blender. Peanut butter is just as good and saves a lot of trouble.

Cooked Chutney

The vegetables for cooked chutney do not have to be perfect, and it is often possible to obtain slightly bruised or spotted aubergines or green peppers very cheaply from a greengrocer, and in the late summer or early autumn green tomatoes, ridge cucumbers and windfall apples should be readily available and cheap.

Cut out the damaged parts and make chutney with any

112

such vegetables or fruit. It is even worth making several jars at a time.

When making chutney one must use a certain amount of sugar and vinegar to ensure that it will keep for a few weeks. The addition of half a sulphur dioxide (Campden) tablet, as used in home wine making, to each jar of anything pickled in brine will ensure that it does keep and will not hurt the flavour at all.

The addition of a spoonful or two of black treacle to chutney helps sweeten it, adds a nice rich flavour and darkens it, taking away the sometimes rather revolting yellowish green colour, especially in chutney which does not contain turmeric.

For chutney to eat with curries do NOT cut the vegetables into tiny pieces, or be tempted to put them through a mincer. Chutney containing recognisable chunks of fruit and vegetable which have soaked up the flavours of the spices is much nicer than an indeterminate mush.

It is possible to make chutney out of almost any fruit or vegetable, with the addition of sugar, spices and vinegar and the addition or omission of ingredients such as apples, celery, dates, sultanas, aubergines, cucumbers, marrow, squash, red tomatoes, garlic, green tomatoes, plums, mangoes, lemons, pears, raisins, will not really make that much difference or ruin anything, provided any one ingredient is not too overwhelming. Onions ARE a universal chutney ingredient. What one is really doing is making spicy vinegar jam. Less sugar is used in chutney than in jam, so the keeping properties may not be so good, although the vinegar helps.

To make hotter chutney, add chopped red chillies, or more chilli powder. Even if a chutney does turn out to be extremely hot, it does not matter because only very small amounts are eaten at a time.

Green Pepper Chutney

3 green peppers
1 tspn turmeric
1 dssrtspn dry mustard
1 dssrtspn cumin
1 large onion
3 cloves garlic
½ tspn ground fenugreek

1 tspn chilli powder
1 large slice green ginger
3 oz/75 g brown sugar
½ pint/3 dl vinegar
1 tspn salt
2 tbspn cooking oil

Slice and chop the onions, green peppers and garlic and cook in the oil till soft. Mix all the other ingredients with the vinegar and put the lot in a saucepan with the cooked vegetables. Simmer until the liquid is reduced to a very thick sauce. Cool, bottle and cover. This will keep for some weeks.

Aubergine Chutney

3 aubergines
1 tspn turmeric
1 tspn dry mustard
1 tspn cumin
3 cloves garlic
½ tspn ground fenugreek

1 tspn chilli powder
3 oz/75 g brown sugar
¼ pint/1½ dl vinegar
1 tspn salt
½ pint/3 dl cooking oil,
    preferably mustard oil

Slice and chop the aubergines and sprinkle with turmeric so that they are well covered. Mix all the ingredients except sugar and oil. Cook the aubergines in the oil till brown and soft, drain and put them aside. Cook the spice mixture in the remaining oil for 10 minutes then add the sugar and the aubergine pieces and simmer until the liquid has turned to a very thick sauce. Cool and bottle and cover immediately. This chutney will keep for some time – up to six months.

Green Tomato Chutney

A very good chutney for those who do not like it too hot.

2 lb/1 kg green tomatoes
1 large onion
3 cloves garlic
2 large cooking apples
2 oz/50 g sultanas or
    chopped dates
1 tspn ground ginger
¼ tspn chilli powder

½ tspn dry mustard
1 tspn salt
1 ridge or ordinary
    cucumber, or a small
    marrow
6 oz/150 g dark brown moist
    sugar
1 pint/6 dl vinegar

Chop the vegetables into small pieces and put all the ingredients together in a saucepan. Bring them to the boil and then simmer till the liquid has turned to a very thick sauce and the pieces of tomato have become translucent. The apple and cucumber will have formed a pulp and gone into the sauce. Bottle when cool, and cover. This chutney will keep for up to six months, though will probably be eaten up long before then.

Sweet Lime or Lemon Chutney

A very popular hot chutney, easy enough to make. Limes are a lot more expensive than lemons and either make a satisfactory chutney.

10 lemons or 15 limes
    (usually smaller than
    lemons)
salt
½ pint/3 dl vinegar
3 oz/75 g raisins or sultanas
1 slice green ginger

2 cloves garlic
2-4 red chillies, depending
    on how hot you like it
1 dssrtspn mustard seed
2 oz/50 g dark brown moist
    sugar

Divide the fruit into quarters and rub the flesh with salt.

Leave the fruit on a plate in a sunny window for 3 or 4 days, turning so that all sides dry out. Or dry them in a very slow oven.

Remove all the pips. Mix together the vinegar and all the other ingredients. Chop eight of the lemon quarters into dice and put them in a saucepan. Put the rest of the fruit and vinegar mixture in a blender and grind them together. Add this mixture to the saucepan with the diced lemon and cook very slowly until the lemon is fairly soft and the sauce is very thick. Cool and bottle.

Ready-Made Chutneys and Pickles

There are several dozen different types of ready-made chutneys and pickles on the market, and one or two firms who specialise in them. These are quite different from the over-vinegared, over-salted, indeterminate chopped vegetables which go under the name of chutney from the shelves of the ordinary grocer's shop, which may be fine with cold meat but are NOT suitable to eat with curries. The true chutneys are really small curries in themselves, cooked to keep, using the same spices, and designed to enhance the flavour of curry dishes.

Ready-made chutneys tend to be pretty hot, even those which are labelled 'mild' are hot to our taste, and the 'hot' ones can be very hot indeed. One does not usually take more than a small spoonful at a time, so the chutneys, though expensive, last a long time. A word of warning here: once opened, some of them do not keep for more than a few weeks, so always buy the smallest jars available.

To Western tastes, sweet mango chutney or sweet plum, which are not hot at all, are excellent accompaniments to any meat curry, and one of them should always be served. There are lime pickles and lemon pickles, both mild and hot, and these have a sharp flavour. Brinjal pickle, made basically from aubergines, is usually medium hot. It is rich and full of flavour, and is a great favourite with most curry eaters. Ballichong or Ballichew (spelt in various ways) is a hot chutney made from shrimps, so is fishy, and certainly

116

adds piquancy to any curry dish. Hot mango chutney is another very full-bodied chutney, usually pretty sweet as well.

Indian Stock or Court Bouillon (Akni)

There are various recipes for this, all made by putting the flavouring ingredients in a muslin bag and suspending them in water and simmering for ½ hour. Vegetarians may use this instead of meat or chicken stock in many recipes.

1 small onion	1 tbspn chopped green
2 cloves garlic	ginger
2 tspn coriander seed	1 chopped green pepper
1 tspn fennel seed	

Make sure all the ingredients are bruised or crushed.

Add to this if you want more flavour:

1 tspn mustard seed	or almost any herbs or spices
a few bay leaves	that you particularly like.
sprigs of parsley, mint or	
lovage.	

Chapter 6

ADVANCED CURRIES – USING WHOLE OR FRESHLY GROUND SPICES AS WELL AS READY-GROUND SPICES AND CURRY POWDERS

No curry is really difficult to make once you have mastered the techniques, although some do contain a great many spices and other ingredients and it is necessary to use most of these. If you have been successful with the curries in earlier chapters then it is worth having a go at some of the ones that follow. More than anything they are time-consuming, and a little fiddly, and some skill is required to achieve the right textures and consistencies of sauce etc. While many of the recipes include ground spices we have now got to the stage where fresh or whole spices ground or prepared for each dish are the best. Because these dishes contain so many ingredients, they are, with a few small side dishes, a feast in themselves. Pilaus particularly, in which the rice is included in the main dish, are wonderful for serving at curry parties or where a large central mountain of food is needed. Just double up quantities for greater numbers.

Coconut and Vegetable Soup for Six

1½ lb/675 g vegetables
   (bamboo shoots,
   courgettes, aubergines,
   French or runner beans,
   peas, cabbage, peanuts,
   etc)
1 tomato
1 tbspn shrimps or prawns
¾ pint/4½ dl thin coconut
   milk (see page 31)
½ pint/3 dl thick coconut
   milk (see page 31)
1 tspn chilli powder
1 onion
1 slice terassi or 1 tspn
   anchovy sauce
2 cloves garlic
½ tspn laos powder (optional)
½ tspn moist dark brown
   sugar
salt to taste
cooking oil

Mix the chopped onion and garlic with the chilli powder,
prawns, terassi or anchovy paste, and fry in a little oil in a
heavy pan for 5 minutes, then add the skinned and chopped
tomato. Cook for another 3 minutes. Add the thin coconut
milk and laos, and bring it to the boil. Add the diced
vegetables, and cook until they are tender. Stir in the thick
coconut milk, add sugar and salt to taste, and serve it piping
hot.

Chicken Mulligatawny Special for Six

1 boiling fowl, or its
   equivalent in chicken
   pieces
3 pints water
8 tbspn butter
salt
1 large onion
1 tbspn curry powder
1 tbspn plain flour
2 cooking apples
1 green pepper
2 stalks of celery
2 carrots
2 cloves
1 tspn ground mace
black pepper
1½ lb/225 g tin tomatoes
4 oz/100 g plain boiled rice
1 tspn brown sugar

Boil the chicken and remove the flesh from the bones. Put the carcass back in the stock and simmer it until you have about 1½ pints/9 dl thick chicken stock, which should jellify if left to cool in the fridge. Melt the butter in a pan, and brown the chicken meat. Chop the onion and brown this in the same butter. Remove the meat and onion, add the curry powder and flour and fry till the pungent smell of curry rises. Then add the sugar, stock and onion, stirring all the time. Chop the remaining vegetables and add them with the rest of the ingredients except the chicken and rice. Simmer for ½ hour, then liquidise. Reheat, add the chicken and serve with rice in a separate dish. This is really a thin curried chicken stew, and is a meal in itself.

Special Spinach (Sagh or Saag)

1 lb/450 g spinach	½ tspn chilli powder
1 large onion	½ tspn salt
½ lb/225 g potatoes	½ tspn ground coriander
1 green chilli (not essential)	3 crushed cardamom seeds
small tin of tomatoes, or	2 tspn fenugreek
4 skinned tomatoes	3 slices green ginger or
½ tspn coriander seeds	2 tspn ground ginger
½ tspn cumin seeds	4 tbspn butter

Slice half the onion and fry it in the butter with the coriander and cumin seeds. In a blender liquidise the rest of the onion with the chilli and coriander. Add these to the onions in the pan and continue cooking for 5 minutes.

Meanwhile wash the spinach and remove all the big ribs with scissors. Chop it and cook it in a saucepan, with a little water to moisten the bottom, till it begins to soften. Clean the potatoes and dice them, and cook them for 5 minutes in salted water. Then put all the ingredients except the tomatoes, potatoes and ginger in a saucepan and simmer over a low flame for 10 minutes.

Brown the potatoes in butter and add with the tomatoes and ginger; simmer again for 20 minutes, turn up the heat and evaporate any remaining liquid, and serve.

To make a really rich vegetable, don't add the potatoes but transfer the rest to an electric casserole or heavy oven casserole and cook as slowly as possible for at least another couple of hours. Fry the potatoes and add 20 minutes before serving. The mixture will be very buttery and rich when served.

Whichever way you cook this mixture, be sure that it comes to the table with all liquid evaporated. The potatoes should be tender, but the mixture not dried out or shrivelled up in any way.

Special Lamb Pilau

This one takes time and trouble, but is well worth it if properly made. The art is to produce this dish with the rice dry and separate, and the lamb well cooked through. For such a recipe it is impossible to give absolutely accurate times for cooking because of variables such as oven heat. This is where your talents as a curry cook come into play.

1 lb/450 g lean lamb	4 oz/100 g butter
½ lb/225 g rice	4 cloves
2 tbspn lime juice	6 cardamom pods
¼ tspn ground aniseed or fennel seed (very different in flavour so it is a matter of personal taste)	2 inches cinnamon stick
	2 tbspn poppy seed
	2 bay leaves
	salt
¼ pint/1½ dl whipped cream	1 bunch watercress
1 carton natural yoghurt or home made (see page 144)	water

Use the bones from the lamb to make a stock. Cover the bones with water and add:

1 piece of lemon rind (yellow part only)	1 tspn peppercorns
1 small green pepper	1 inch chopped green ginger

Simmer this for an hour till the liquid is reduced to about a cupful. Leave it to cool and take off any fat.

Wash the rice thoroughly and leave it to soak for 1 hour. Cube the meat and dry it thoroughly. Prick it all over and then mix together the lime juice and aniseed or fennel seed and rub this all over the meat, making sure it is well coated. Put the cream and yoghurt into a basin and stir the meat into this.

Bruise the cardamoms and cloves, and break up the cinnamon stick. Roast the poppy seeds in a dry tin and then grind or crush them. Heat the butter, add the spices and after 1 minute add the reduced stock. Cover and cook over a low flame for 5 minutes, evaporating away most of the stock. Add the rice to this and continue to cook, stirring occasionally for about 8 minutes, until the rice has absorbed the butter and become translucent. Strain the marinade from the meat on to this and add enough water just to cover the rice by 1¼ inches. Bring this to the boil but do not stir again, and add the chopped watercress. Cook gently without stirring till the rice is just done.

While the rice is finishing, fry the lamb in butter and when it is nicely browned, transfer the cooked rice to an oven dish and pile the meat on top of it. Cover and place in a slow oven for ½ hour. This will steam the meat and further cook it, and should serve to evaporate any remaining liquid so that the rice is dry and separate.

Should there still be liquid in the rice, remove the cover and allow it to steam for a few minutes longer.

Indonesian Rice with Pork and Shrimps (Nasi Goreng)

This is a standard recipe capable of variation according to ingredients available, and provided the spices are all in there, the other ingredients may be included or omitted as desired.

1 lb/450 g rice
1 dssrtspn moist brown
    sugar
1 dssrtspn coriander
1 tspn cumin
1 bay leaf
salt
pinch of laos (not essential)
2-4 red chillies (according to
    hotness required) or
    $\frac{1}{2}$ tspn chilli powder

$\frac{1}{2}$ tspn terassi or anchovy
    sauce
2 large onions
2 cloves garlic
2 oz/50 g shrimps or prawns
    (more if liked)
$\frac{1}{2}$ lb cooked, diced pork, or
    $\frac{1}{2}$ lb/225 g chopped bacon
1 tbspn butter
2 eggs
spring onions or chives

Boil the rice according to Method 1 or 2 (see page 61) drain it and leave it to cool, overnight if possible. Fry the shrimps in butter till just golden, remove them and then fry the pork or bacon in the same butter. Put the pieces aside while you fry together the chopped onions, garlic, chillies, coriander, cumin, brown sugar, terassi and laos with the bay leaf and a little salt in the fat drained from the meat and shrimps. Add a little more butter if necessary. When this concoction is blended and the onions soft, combine them with the meat and shrimps and the cooked rice, and heat everything together for a few minutes.

Serve topped with an omelette cut into strips, chopped chives or spring onions, and some lightly steamed bean sprouts (see page 67). Serve roasted or fried peanuts as a side dish, and soy sauce.

Special Nasi Goreng

To the previous recipe add, with the shrimp and pork:

cooked chicken meat cut
into small pieces, lightly
fried in butter

crab or lobster meat, fried in
butter

Hot Vegetables with Peanut Sauce (Gado Gado)

This makes a big dish of vegetables, enough for at least
four people, or up to eight if several other curry dishes are
being served.

Peanut sauce No. 5 as per recipe on page 112.
$\frac{1}{2}$ lb/225 g bean sprouts
1 small white cabbage
$\frac{1}{4}$ lb/100 g green peas
$\frac{1}{2}$ lb/225 g French beans
$\frac{1}{2}$ lb/225 g potatoes (new if
possible)

1 cucumber
$\frac{1}{2}$ pint/3 dl thick coconut
milk (see page 31)
2 large onions
1 clove garlic
cooking oil

Shred the cabbage and put it and the beans, peas and bean
sprouts into a steamer, keeping them separate, and steam
them until the vegetables are done but not mushy, which
will take less than 15 minutes. Cook the potatoes till just
done, and slice them. Slice the onions and garlic and fry
them in a little oil. Drain. Slice the cucumber and arrange
the pieces in a ring on a big dish. Fill the middle with the
sliced potatoes and carefully place the steamed vegetables
in layers on the bed of potatoes. Heat the thick coconut
milk, mix it with the peanut sauce and simmer until it is
fairly thick. Pour this all over the hot vegetables. Serve
immediately garnished with strips of omelette and the fried
onions and garlic.

The vegetables used for this dish may be varied. Sliced

124

and lightly boiled carrots may be included, and the quantities of peas and beans altered. Broad beans can be included and cauliflower substituted for the cabbage.

It is a wonderful accompaniment for any curry, and specially if a lot of people are to be served as it combines many ingredients into one dish. Double up the total quantities if necessary.

Chicken Pilau (Rabbit, Lamb or Pork)

This recipe will take some time to make as it requires two separate recipes to be followed and then combined. However it is excellent for a dinner party or curry party. It can be made with lamb, pork or rabbit instead of chicken.

1½ lb/675 g chicken pieces (or rabbit, lamb or pork)
½ tspn ground ginger
½ tspn cardamom
1 green pepper
1 large onion
2 cloves garlic
1 tbspn raisins
1 tbspn coriander

1 tbspn cumin
1 bay leaf
1 tbspn blanched almonds
2 tbspn butter
1 carton natural yoghurt, or home made (see page 144)
1 red chilli or ½ tspn chilli powder
juice of 1 lemon

For the Rice:
½ lb/225 g rice
1 tbspn butter
½ tspn ground cardamom
grated nutmeg
1 bay leaf
1 tbspn sultanas

1 tbspn blanched almonds
1 onion
1 tbspn chopped parsley
1 tspn salt
chicken stock

Skin the chicken portions and prick them all over. Mix together the minced onions and chopped and seeded green pepper and chilli if used, with the bay leaf, chopped almonds and all the spices, and rub this on to the chicken and leave for at least 1 hour to marinate. Then fry the chicken pieces

125

in the butter with the marinade and when they are lightly browned, add the yoghurt, fry for another 5 minutes, and add the lemon juice. Then cook very slowly in a covered pan till the meat is tender and can be removed from the bones. If the contents of the pan get too dry, just add a little water. The final sauce should be thick and creamy.

Wash the rice thoroughly. Fry it in the butter till translucent then add the spices and bay leaf and a dash of nutmeg. Mix in the contents of the other saucepan and add the sultanas. Transfer the lot to a fireproof casserole or dish in which it can be served. Add enough chicken stock to cover the rice by 1½ inches, and cook in a low heat until the rice is done, without stirring.

Fry the sliced onion in butter till brown, and sprinkle the top of the pilau with almonds and onions and chopped parsley.

Replace the lid and cook very slowly in a low oven for 10 minutes and serve immediately.

Serves 6–8 people

Whole Chicken and Lamb Pilau

This rather special pilau will take some time to make and is ideal for a special curry dinner or even as the centre for a curry party. If you succeed then you really are a good curry cook!

1 large chicken	¼ tspn saffron
1½ lb/675 lean lamb	2 bay leaves
4 eggs	4 tbspn ground coriander
1 lb/450 g rice	4 cloves
½ lb/225 g butter	2 tspn ground ginger
3 large onions	½ tspn chilli powder
4 tbspn chick pea flour, or 2 tbspn plain flour and 1 tbspn cornflour	4 oz/100 g blanched almonds
1 tspn black pepper	2 oz/50 g shelled pistachios if available, or extra almonds
1 tspn salt	2 oz raisins
1 tspn ground cardamom	small carton natural yoghurt,
½ tspn ground cinnamon or 1-inch stick	or home made (see page 144)

Slice, chop and cook two of the onions in a tablespoonful of the butter till soft and golden. Mince half the lamb and put it into an oven dish with a lid and cook in a slow oven for ¾ hour; pour off the fat. Blend in to the meat the separated and lightly beaten egg whites, the cooked onion, flour, black pepper and crumbled bay leaf. Pound or blend together the nuts and raisins, salt, coriander and saffron with a dessertspoonful of yoghurt and mix this into the meat. Form this mixture into little golf balls with your hands, and fry them in butter till brown.

Cut the rest of the lamb into dice and fry it in butter with salt and half the chilli powder.

Skin the chicken and prick it all over with a knife. Rub well into it a paste made of the other onion chopped very finely, half the ground ginger, and half the ground cardamom. Stuff the chicken with the diced lamb, pour the rest of the yoghurt over it and roast it in a covered tin, basting frequently with the yoghurt and juice till done.

Fry the rice in the remaining butter with the rest of the cardamom, the cloves and cinnamon. When it is translucent, add the bay leaf, the rest of the ginger and coriander. Take all the dish gravy from the chicken and add this to the rice. Put the chicken in a casserole large enough to take everything; surround it with the rice; pour on enough water or chicken stock to cover the rice by 1 inch, put the meat balls round the chicken on the rice. Cook the whole lot covered in a slow to medium oven till the liquid is absorbed and the rice is tender. Add a little more liquid if necessary.

When cooked arrange all the food on a big dish with the chicken in the middle.

Beat the egg yolks with a little salt and pepper, the rest of the chilli powder and make an omelette. Cut it into strips and use it to garnish the pilau.

If you wish to make more omelette, just add 1 egg per person, and make several small omelettes instead of one big one, and serve them whole, not cut into strips.

Serves 8 people

Special Chicken Curry

Use the spice seeds for this curry to get the very best result, which is extremely tasty, but need not be desperately hot.

1 chicken
2 tspn turmeric
1 tspn ground chilli powder
1-inch slice green ginger, or
   1 tspn ground ginger
2 curry leaves or bay leaves
1 stalk lemon grass
2 cloves garlic
1 large onion
1 tspn coriander seeds
½ tspn cumin seeds
¼ tspn fennel seeds
¼ tspn mustard seeds
¼ tspn fenugreek seeds
4 cardamom pods or ¼ tspn
   ground cardamom

¼ tspn salt
2 tspn brown sugar
1½ pints/9 dl medium
   coconut milk
2 tbspn lemon or lime juice
cooking oil

or 1 dssrtspn Ceylon curry powder

Cut the chicken into serving pieces and rub them all over with turmeric and salt. Put a tablespoonful of oil in a heavy pan and fry the seeds in this until pungent, with the lemon grass and curry leaves. Grind the cooked mixture to a paste in a blender or a mortar. If using curry powder, cook the powder with the curry leaves and lemon grass in the oil.

Put two thirds of the coconut milk in a saucepan with all the other ingredients, except the lemon juice, including the chicken and cooked spices and simmer uncovered till the chicken is tender. Add the rest of the coconut milk and cook till the sauce is fairly thick. Stir in the lemon juice and serve with any rice – plain, yellow or saffron.

Nutty Mutton Curry

As its name implies, a rich and flavoursome curry.

1½ lb/675 g lean mutton or
   lamb
4 tbspn cashew nuts
2 oz/150 g desiccated
   coconut
2 tbspn blanched almonds
¼ tspn ground ginger
1 tspn turmeric
1 tbspn poppy seeds
1 tbspn ground fenugreek
2 tbspn sesame seeds

½ tspn chilli powder
1 tspn black pepper
4 tbspn butter or ghee
2 large onions
3 cloves garlic
4 tbspn lime or lemon juice
¼ pint/1½ dl thin coconut
   milk (see page 31)
1 tspn salt
6 cloves

Make a paste by blending together all the nuts (including coconut) with a little coconut milk. Mix together the poppy seeds, sesame seeds, fenugreek, ginger, black pepper, turmeric, chilli and cloves.

Cube the mutton and cook it in the heated butter with the finely chopped onions till brown, for about 10 minutes, then add the mixture of spices and continue to fry for another 5 minutes. Add a little water to cover the meat and bring to the boil. Add half the lemon juice and the crushed garlic and the nut paste, stir thoroughly, and cook over a low heat until the meat is tender and the liquid reduced to a very thick sauce. Add the rest of the coconut milk and cook again for 20 minutes till the sauce is thick; add the rest of the lemon juice and serve with rice and poppadums.

Lamb Biriani

A little complicated, but a lovely curry.

1½ lb/675 g lean lamb
3 large onions
3 cloves garlic
1 tspn ground coriander
¼ tspn ground cloves
¼ tspn ground cardamom
¼ tspn chilli powder
¼ tspn cinnamon
¼ tspn black pepper
3 slices green ginger, or
   1 tspn ground ginger
2 oz/50 g raisins
2 oz/50 g blanched almonds
1 green chilli
1 green pepper

1 carton natural yoghurt, or
   home made (see page
   144)
6 oz/150 g butter
1 tspn salt
   home made (see page 144)
For the Rice:
½ lb/225 g rice
2 tspn salt
3 bay leaves
3 inches cinnamon stick
5 whole cardamoms
5 whole peppercorns
½ tspn saffron
1 dssrtspn hot milk

Dice the meat and put it in a pan with the spices. Fry till well blended in half the butter, then put aside and add the lemon juice, yoghurt, raisins and salt. Mix well, and leave to stand while you prepare the rest of the food. Slice the onions and crush the garlic. Slice and chop the green pepper, the chilli and the ginger. (If using ground ginger that will already be in with the meat.) Cook the onions and other vegetables in the rest of the butter till soft.

Wash the rice thoroughly and put it in a saucepan with all the rice ingredients except the saffron and milk, and fill the saucepan with boiling water so that the rice is covered by at least 2 inches. Cook for 5 minutes, then drain. Mix the saffron with the hot milk and 4 oz/100 g butter. Mix together the meat and vegetables and put them in the bottom of a big saucepan. Put the rice on top and pour the milk, butter and saffron mixture all over. Put on a tight fitting lid and cook over an extremely low flame for 1½ hours.

131

Alternatively, food can be put into a slow-cooking electric casserole and cooked for at least 2 hours, or in an oven proof dish or casserole and cooked standing in a shallow tray of boiling water for at least 2 hours.

To serve the biriani, remove the rice, put the meat mixture on a very hot dish, pile the rice on top and garnish with slices of hard-boiled egg and the blanched almonds sprinkled on top. A few plain accompaniments and chutneys are all that is needed with this very rich and tasty curry.

Javanese Beef Curry

1 lb/450 g stewing steak
¼ small tight green cabbage
2 tspn ground coriander
½ tspn ground cumin
1 tspn chilli powder
½ tspn turmeric
1 tspn terassi or anchovy sauce
3 cloves garlic
1 large onion
1 slice green ginger or 1 tspn ground ginger

3 brazil nuts or walnuts
½ tspn laos powder (not essential)
3 curry leaves or bay leaves
1 stem lemon grass or 1 slice yellow lemon peel
¼ pint/1½ dl thick coconut milk
salt to taste
½ lb/225 g new potatoes or tin of potatoes
cooking oil

Mix together the spices, terassi, nuts, ginger and garlic with the chopped onion. With a little oil grind them together in a blender and then fry them in a pan till pungent. Dice the beef into a pan and add the paste, laos, bay leaves, lemon grass and salt. Just cover with water and simmer with a lid on until the meat is tender. Add the potatoes, and when they are just cooked, the chopped cabbage and the coconut milk. Stir everything, correct the seasoning with salt and lemon juice and serve at once with lots of rice or bread as this is a curry with plenty of liquid.

Indonesian Beef Slices

An Eastern version of pepper steak.

1 lb/450 g topside steak	1-inch cinnamon stick
2 large onions	2 tomatoes
3 cloves garlic	1 tbspn butter
3 tbspn soy sauce	1 tspn ground black pepper
1 tbspn brown sugar	

Slice the meat into small pieces and then beat them out very thinly with a steak mallet. Mince one onion and garlic and make them into a paste in a blender with the pepper, sugar and soy sauce. Spread this paste all over the meat slices and leave them for up to 1 hour.

Fry the other sliced onion in oil until it is soft and then add the meat slices and marinade. Fry them until browned (about 8 minutes), stirring and turning them so that they do not overcook. Add the cinnamon. Skin the tomatoes and chop them in with the meat, adding just enough water to cover. Simmer uncovered until the meat is tender and most of the liquid has gone.

This dish is excellent served with any type of rice, or the slices can be lightly grilled till just crisp and served with any hot relish as a curry accompaniment at a dinner or curry party.

This recipe has been included as advanced because it takes practice to get the meat cooked just right – not too tender, not too dry.

Crab Meat Balls

Delicious and excellent for parties.

½ lb/225 g crab or lobster
  meat
1 tspn parsley
1 tspn mint
1 tspn tarragon or basil
1 tspn lemon grass or balm
  (melissa)
3 bay leaves
1 large onion
1 clove garlic

1 tspn ground coriander
½ tspn ground cumin
½ tspn ground ginger
1 red chilli
½ tspn black pepper
½ tspn garam masala
4 tbspn tomato juice
4 tbspn breadcrumbs
1 egg
4 tbspn butter or mustard oil

Break up the crab meat with a fork till it is completely shredded. Chop the herbs except the lemon grass and bay leaves and mix them with the meat. Add the spices, except the garam masala, and mix thoroughly with enough tomato juice to make it possible to mould the mixture into little golf balls. Dip these in the beaten egg and roll them in breadcrumbs.

Chop the onions and chillies and garlic and fry them with the lemon grass, garam masala and crumbled bay leaves until golden. Add the crab balls carefully and continue to cook till the outsides are also crisp and golden brown. Serve at once with plain boiled rice, lemon wedges, cucumber slices and hard-boiled egg slices as garnish.

White Fish Steamed with Herbs and Spices

1 lb/450 g white fish, filleted
2 tbspn cooking oil
1 tbspn ground coriander
1 tbspn dill seed
2 tbspn cornflour
1 tspn ground ginger
1 carton natural yoghurt, or
    home made (see page 144)

½ tspn ground cardamom
¼ tspn ground saffron
1 tbspn chopped fresh mint
1 small cucumber
½ tspn salt
¼ tspn ground cinnamon
1 tspn sesame seeds
2 tbspn butter

Skin the fish and cut it into small steaks. Mix together the
oil, ground coriander, ginger, cinnamon, cornflour, dill, and
sesame seeds, and spread this all over the fish, rubbing it in
well. Leave for ½ hour. Meanwhile pound together the
onions and cardamom and mix with half the yoghurt, spread
this also over the fish. Leave for a further ¼ hour while you
pound together the mint with the rest of the yoghurt and
the saffron and salt. Put the marinaded fish in a saucepan,
pour the mint, yoghurt and saffron mixture over it and cook
it over a low flame with the cucumber cut into big chunks,
till the marinade has nearly all dried out, about 10 minutes.
Turn the fish once. Then carefully remove the contents of
the saucepan to a lidded ovenproof dish, and put chunks of
butter all over the fish before putting on the lid and cooking
the whole lot for another 15 minutes in a medium oven.

Grilled Spicy Duck

This recipe can be used for any poultry or game.

1 duck
1 tbspn ground coriander
1 tbspn ground cumin
1 tbspn fennel seeds
1 tspn ground turmeric
1 tspn ground nutmeg
2-inch piece of cinnamon or
   $\frac{1}{2}$ tspn ground cinnamon
4 cloves
$\frac{1}{2}$ tspn ground cardamom
$\frac{1}{2}$ tspn ground black pepper

1 piece green ginger, or
   1 tspn ground ginger
1 stalk lemon grass, or
   1 tbspn lemon juice
2 onions
1 clove garlic
1 fresh chilli or $\frac{1}{2}$ tspn chilli
   powder
$\frac{1}{4}$ pint/$1\frac{1}{2}$ dl coconut milk
1 sharp cooking apple

Joint and skin the duck. Mix together all the other ingredients, having chopped the onions and garlic, and put them through a blender till you have a thick paste. Coat the duck with the paste, and grill or barbecue, turning frequently and putting on more of the spiced paste as the duck cooks. A modern electric rotisserie will also serve very well to cook duck prepared this way, or it can be done on a rack over a pan in a fairly hot oven, but this means continually opening the oven to baste the duck.

This is absolutely delicious and should be served with plain boiled rice.

Eggs in Turmeric

A most useful recipe as these eggs go with almost any curry, or, with rice and a curry sauce, are a meal in themselves.

8 large eggs
1 tspn turmeric
½ tspn salt
cooking oil

For the sauce:
1 small onion
2 cloves garlic
1 slice green ginger or ½ tspn ground ginger
1 stem lemon grass (optional)
3 bay leaves
pinch of fennel seeds

3 tspn coriander seeds or 1 tspn ground coriander
½ tspn fenugreek seeds or ground fenugreek
1 tspn cumin seeds, or ½ tspn ground cumin
2 tbspn lemon juice
½ pint/3 dl coconut milk
1 red chilli or ¼ tspn chilli powder
1 tbspn butter
1 tspn terassi or anchovy sauce

Hard boil the eggs, shell them and prick them all over with a fork. When they are cool, roll them in the turmeric and salt spread out on a plate, then fry them in butter till they turn ginger.

Fry together the chopped onion and garlic and the lemon grass and crumbled bay leaves for 5 minutes, till the onion is soft. Then add the other ingredients except the lemon juice, and cook very slowly until it is well blended and has reduced to a thick sauce. Add the lemon juice and the eggs, cook for another 10 minutes until the eggs are heated through, and serve on plain boiled rice.

Made with whole spices, this sauce will be a little nutty and gritty; made with ground spices it should be very smooth.

Chapter 7

COOKED DESSERTS, YOGHURT, ICE CREAMS, FRUIT AND FRUIT SALADS, DRINKS

Indian desserts are on the whole far too sweet and sickly for Western tastes; however I have included several sweet rice recipes. Use Patna rice, not 'pudding rice' as sold here. Any kind of water ice or sorbet or dessert made with fresh fruit follows curries well but nothing too rich or heavy. Whatever is cool and refreshing goes well.

Sweet Rice

½ lb/225 g Patna rice
4 oz/100 g candied orange peel
4 oz/100 g sultanas
2 oz/50 g blanched and chopped almonds

2 oz/50 g crystallised cherries
Few pieces of angelica
2 tbspn cooking oil

Cook the rice and when done divide it into three parts. Also divide the orange peel, sultanas and almonds into three. Put one portion of the rice into an ovenproof dish with a lid. Cover with a layer of fruit and nuts and repeat the layers until the ingredients are used up. Pour the oil carefully into the dish and turn it all ways so that the sides and bottom are all coated. Put a piece of cooking foil over the top and cover with the lid. Bake in a slow oven for 3 hours, and serve sprinkled with chopped crystallised cherries and angelica.

Sweet Pilau

½ lb/225 g Patna rice	1 blade mace or ½ tspn
3 cloves	ground mace
pinch ground cardamom	1 tsp cinnamon powder or 2
2 oz/50 g sultanas	inches cinnamon stick
2 oz/50 g blanched almonds	pinch dried saffron
or pistachio nuts	pinch salt
1 tbspn brown moist sugar	1 tbspn butter

Brown the well washed rice in the melted butter and then add all the spices and sugar and salt and stir over the heat for a minute; do not burn. Cover with water, bring to the boil and then simmer very gently with a lid on until the rice is tender. Add a little more water if necessary. Add the sultanas and nuts just a few minutes before serving.

Rice and Coconut Pudding

½ lb/225 g Patna rice	4 oz/100 g fresh or
1½ pints/9 dl water	desiccated coconut
½ tspn salt	2 tspn grated lemon rind
4 oz/100 g sugar	1 tspn ground cinnamon
	¼ pint/1½ dl milk

Wash the rice and then cook it in the water and salt for 15 minutes. Drain off the rest of the water and put the rice back in the pan with the sugar, coconut and milk. Cook over a very low heat for 15 minutes, stirring all the time until the milk has been absorbed. Add the lemon rind, mix it in and tip the mixture into a serving bowl and sprinkle with cinnamon. Serve either hot or cooled in the fridge.

Lime and Sesame Meringue

This is a delicious kind of sweet and sharp soufflé.

2 limes or 3 tbspn lime juice	2 oz/50 g sesame seeds
4 oz/100 g moist brown sugar	4 eggs
	pinch saffron
2 oz/50 g butter	2 drops almond essence

Cream the butter and sugar together and add the lime juice and the beaten yolks of the eggs. Mix well and add the saffron and almond essence. Roast the sesame seeds in a shallow dish in a hot oven until they are golden brown and then add them to the mixture. Put all this into a double saucepan and heat it over boiling water until it thickens, stirring all the time. Do not let it boil. Remove it from the heat and spoon the mixture into a shallow baking dish, fold in the stiffly beaten egg whites, and cook for about 20 minutes in a slow oven. Serve hot.

Caramel Custard

Caramel ingredients:
3 oz/75 g granulated sugar
3 tbspn water

Custard ingredients:
4 eggs
2 oz/50 g caster sugar
1 pint/6 dl milk
vanilla essence

Dissolve the granulated sugar in the water, then bring it to the boil and cook until it is golden brown. Pour the caramel evenly into the moulds and, when cool, butter the sides of the moulds above the liquid.

Mix the eggs and caster sugar well. Warm the milk and add it to the egg mixture with a few drops of vanilla essence. Pour this on to the caramel in the moulds and put the dishes in an oven tray half filled with hot water. Bake in a slow oven for 1 hour. Leave the custards to cool overnight before turning them out into individual serving dishes.

Orange Pudding

4 oz/100 g sugar	1¼ pints/7½ dl orange juice
5 tbspn cornflour	3 eggs
pinch salt	2 tspn lemon juice

Mix the sugar, cornflour and salt in a double saucepan and add the warmed orange juice. Cook, stirring constantly, until the mixture is thick, then remove it from the heat. Separate the eggs. Beat the yolks and add them slowly to the sauce, mixing them well in. Cook in the double saucepan for another few minutes, stirring constantly. The mixture must not be allowed to boil; as soon as it thickens remove it from the heat. Add the lemon juice, allow the mixture to cool and carefully fold in the stiffly beaten egg whites. Pour it into individual dishes and serve well chilled.

Banana Pudding

3 eggs	4 oz/100 g sugar
½ tbspn vanilla essence or	½ pint/3 dl milk
½ powdered vanilla pod	3 bananas

Beat the vanilla into the eggs, add the sugar and milk and stir well. Add the thinly sliced bananas and cook either by steaming in a pudding basin, or in a shallow dish standing in another dish of water, for about ½ hour in a medium oven.

Banana Fritters

4 ripe bananas
3 tbspn plain flour
½ tspn salt
3 tbspn caster sugar

cooking oil
1 dssrtspn icing sugar
½ tspn ground cinnamon

Mash together the bananas, flour, salt and sugar, till a little frothy. A blender will do this well. Heat the oil till just smoking and drop the fritter mixture in a tablespoonful at a time. Cook, turning once, till brown on both sides. Drain and serve at once. Sprinkle with the icing sugar and cinnamon mixed together.

Banana Halva

6 large ripe bananas
2 tbspn butter
⅓ pint/2 dl water
4 tbspn sugar
pinch nutmeg

pinch cardamom
few drops almond essence
2 tbspn blanched and
    chopped almonds

Peel the bananas, slice them thinly and fry them in the butter in a non-stick frying pan for 5 minutes until they are soft. Mash or liquidise them, adding three or four spoonsful of water. Reheat and stir constantly for another couple of minutes. Dissolve the sugar in the rest of the water and pour it into the banana mush. Simmer gently for about 10 minutes to make the mixture smooth, and when it is quite thick, turn it into a bowl. When it has cooled a little add the almond essence, and whisk it until it is light and fluffy. Carefully fold in the nutmeg, cardamom and chopped almonds. Cool in the fridge before serving with cream. This is a cream dessert rather than a pudding.

Banana Cream for Two

2 or 3 bananas
1 small carton plain yoghurt, or home made (see page 144)

2 tbspn double cream
1 dssrtspn caster sugar
2 egg whites

Mash the bananas thoroughly and then mix them with the yoghurt, cream and sugar. Whip the egg whites until they are quite stiff and fold them into the mixture. Serve this well chilled. If it is left too long, the pudding will separate out, but can be whisked again just before serving.

Banana and Orange Whip

The quantities in this recipe are for one person, but can be increased in proportion for as many as you like.

1 banana
2 dssrtspn orange juice

1 dssrtspn double cream
1 tspn caster sugar

Mash the banana, add the orange juice, stir well, then add the cream. Add the sugar and serve instantly.

Lemon Froth

6 eggs
6 oz/150 g white sugar
¼ packet lemon jelly cubes
¼ pint/1½ dl boiling water

¼ pint/1½ dl fresh lemon juice
1 tspn grated lemon rind

Separate the eggs and beat the yolks thoroughly, gradually adding the sugar. Dissolve the jelly cubes in the boiling water, then add the lemon juice and grated rind, allow to cool a little and beat this into the yolks. When the mixture has begun to set, beat the egg whites until very stiff, whip up the yolk

143

mixture and fold it into the whites. Put into individual serving dishes and leave it in the fridge until it is very cold and firmly set.

Natural Yoghurt

1 pint milk
2 tbspn dried milk powder
1 tbspn caster sugar

½ carton natural yoghurt for
  starter

To make your own yoghurt you need a wide necked vacuum flask and a cooking thermometer. No other special equipment is necessary.

Heat the milk to 114°F (45°C). Warm the flask with hot water. Add the milk powder, sugar and yoghurt and transfer everything immediately to the warmed flask. Put on the lid tightly, and leave it for 12 hours. Keep back half a carton of this yoghurt to use as starter next time. It will deep freeze perfectly if required, but thaw it out to room temperature before use, or it will cool down the warmed milk and the yoghurt will not 'make'.

This yoghurt can be made without sugar and used to add to various curry recipes, although even with sugar it is perfectly suitable as an addition. To make flavoured yoghurts just mix in spoonsful of jam, nuts, fruit syrup, chocolate, coffee, etc to taste.

Persimmon Ice Cream

4 ripe persimmons
2 tbspn sugar

5 tbspn lemon juice
¾ pint/4½ dl double cream

Put the flesh only of the fruit through an electric blender then beat it with the sugar and lemon juice. Whip the cream stiffly and fold in the sugared purée. Pour it into a freezing tray and leave it to set hard.

Orange Water Ice

1½ pint/9 dl water   finely grated rind of 1 orange
¾ pint/4½ dl orange juice   and 1 lemon
¼ pint/1½ dl lemon juice   ¾ lb/325 g sugar

Boil the water and sugar for 5 minutes, then cool it slightly
and add the orange and lemon juice and the grated rinds.
Leave it to cool for a couple of hours, then strain it through
a fine sieve and pour it into a shallow ice tray. Freeze hard
before serving.

Coffee Ice Cream

This makes a very rich ice cream.

2 eggs   2 tbspn coffee essence
2 oz/50 g icing sugar   1 small carton double cream

Separate the eggs and whip the whites stiffly; slowly mix
in the icing sugar. Whip the yolks and coffee essence and
fold them into the whites. Whisk the cream and fold that
in as well.

Pour the mixture into a freezing tray and leave it to set
firmly. Chopped nuts, chocolate chips or lightly crushed
meringue pieces can also be folded in with the cream.

Orange and Lemon Ice

¼ pint/1½ dl orange juice   ½ pint/3 dl milk
⅛ pint/¾ dl lemon juice   1 small tin evaporated milk,
6 oz/150 g sugar   chilled icy cold

Combine the juices and sugar, stir in the milk, pour them
all into a freezer tray and put it in the freezing compartment.

Freeze it until it is firm and then break it into chunks

and beat it in a blender until it is quite smooth. Whip the very cold evaporated milk until it is thick and then fold it into the frozen mixture. Return it to the tray and freeze until it is quite solid.

Simple Grapefruit or Orange Sorbet

6 oz/150 g tin of frozen   ½ pint/3 dl water
   grapefruit or orange juice   1 egg white
6 tbspn caster sugar

Heat the sugar and water until the sugar is dissolved. The amount of sugar can be varied according to taste and for a sharp refreshing orange sorbet not more than two or three spoonsful need be added. Add the concentrated fruit juice, stir well and put the mixture into a shallow dish in the freezing compartment of the fridge. Leave it there for an hour or so until it has formed fairly hard ice crystals. If the fruit juice mixture is not frozen through, the egg will not blend quite so well. Whisk up the egg white stiffly, break up the iced fruit juice with a fork and fold in the egg white. Return the mixture to the freezing compartment and leave it until it comes out as a solid lump which must then be broken with a fork into individual serving portions. Serve it immediately.

This recipe can be made with fresh orange or grapefruit juice, but of course less water will be needed as the total amount of liquid should be only just over ½ pint/3 dl for each egg white.

Fresh Fruit and Fresh Fruit Salads

Fresh fruit or fruit salad cools and refreshes the palate after a hot curry. All the tropical fruits go particularly well, so do apples and pears, peaches and other familiar European fruit, but the delicate and fine flavours of soft fruits such as strawberries and raspberries are completely masked if you have just been eating hot curries and are best avoided.

Fresh Fruit Salad

2 dessert apples
2 dessert pears
2 oranges
2 bananas

½ lb/225 g grapes
2 tbspn lime juice
2 oz/50 g caster sugar
1 tbspn Grand Marnier

Dissolve the sugar in a scant ¼ pint/1½ dl boiling water, and when cool add the lime juice and Grand Marnier. Peel and core the pears and apples and slice them thinly directly into the syrup with the sliced bananas, skinned and de-pipped grapes (see page 148) and the peeled and de-membraned oranges. Stir them gently, and chill before serving with cream.

Any other fruits can be added, so the appearance as well as the taste of this basic fruit salad can be greatly altered by putting in cherries, plums and apricot pieces or a handful of redcurrants.

Indian Fruit Salad (Chaart)

4 mandarin oranges, or 1
    small tin
2 eating apples
2 bananas
2 guavas, or 1 small tin
2 pears
1 good handful stoned
    cherries

2 tbspn lemon juice
2 tbspn caster sugar
1 tspn paprika
¼ tspn chilli powder
¼ tspn salt
1 tspn ground ginger
1 tspn garam masala

Peel and prepare the fruit, removing all pips and stones, and chop them into similar sized pieces. Put all the fruit into a bowl with the lemon juice sprinkled over. Mix the sugar and spices in a different bowl and sprinkle them over the fruit, making sure that it is well scattered around. Chill in the fridge before serving.

The fruit varieties can be altered according to what is

147

available, but keep the proportions about the same so that the sugar and spice quantities remain correct.

Apricots. Fresh apricots are refreshing after curry. Stone them by cutting them in half with a sharp knife round the indentation. Twist the two halves in opposite directions to separate them, then dig out the stone with a sharp knife.

Chinese Gooseberries or Kiwi Fruit. These taste faintly of melon and strawberry and are imported from New Zealand fresh or tinned. They are brown, hairy and about 3 inches long, but when cut the flesh is pale green and seeded and looks very appetising. Ripe fruit are just soft to the touch. They are very pleasant eaten straight, scooped out with a spoon, but are even nicer when served with yoghurt, cream or ice cream. They mix well with other fruit to make a fruit salad. Serve them halved in a dish of crushed ice, or as:

Chinese Gooseberry Chantilly

3 Chinese gooseberries	2 tspn icing sugar
2 tbspn Kirsch	dessert wafers or biscuits
small carton cream	

Peel the fruit and dice it. Sprinkle with Kirsch and leave it in the fridge to marinate for an hour. Sweeten the cream with the icing sugar and whip it till it is buttery. Drain off any liquid from the gooseberries into the cream and mix well. Add a spot more Kirsch if necessary to make it the right consistency. Fold in the gooseberry pieces and serve in individual dishes.

Custard Apple. This fruit has a green lightly bumpy skin and the white flesh is studded with black seeds. Scoop the white flesh out of the skin and discard the pips. It has a light refreshing flavour.

Grapes. These are refreshing after a hot curry, either eaten straight from a bunch, or else mixed in a fresh fruit salad. They are rather a nuisance to prepare, but the easiest way to get rid of the pips is to use the rounded end of a 'kirby-grip' inserted in the hole made by pulling out the stalk.

Grape Jelly

1 lb/450 g white grapes	2 tbspn caster sugar
juice of 2 oranges	4 tbspn water
juice of 1 lemon	1½ tspn powdered gelatine

Put the sugar with half the water in a pan over a low heat and stir until the sugar is dissolved. Warm the rest of the water separately and dissolve the gelatine. Combine the two, stir thoroughly and in it put all the citrus juices, which should make up about ½ pint/3 dl liquid. Leave it to cool until it begins to set.

Peel the grapes by putting them in boiling water for half a minute, then the skins will come off easily and the pips can be scooped out. Put the grapes in a serving bowl and pour the jelly over the top. Put it in the fridge to set firmly before serving.

Grape and Melon Fruit Salad

½ lb/225 g white grapes	½ lb/225 g red grapes
½ lb/225 g honeydew melon chunks	3 tbspn runny honey
	3 tbspn lemon juice
½ lb/225 g watermelon chunks	a few sprigs of mint

The grapes and melon chunks taste just as good simply mixed together, but to appeal to the eye more, scoop little balls from the melon with a special gadget and skin and de-pip the grapes. Mix the honey and the lemon juice and pour them over the fruit. Garnish with a few sprigs of mint and chill well before serving.

149

Grapefruit. Serve cold cut in half with the membrane removed from the cut segments, and sprinkle on a little caster sugar. Or put a dessertspoonful of sherry and a teaspoonful of brown sugar on each prepared half, then heat them gently under the grill. Be sure they do not burn before they are warmed through.

Guavas. These can sometimes be bought fresh, when they should be peeled, sliced, sprinkled with sugar and eaten chilled with cream. Guavas can be bought in tins, with or without seeds, and are excellent added to other fruit in a fruit salad.

Kumquat. These are small elongated oranges which can sometimes be bought fresh, in which case they should be eaten just like ordinary oranges. They are also obtainable in tins.

Kumquat Fruit Salad

1 small tin kumquats
1 small tin pineapple rings
1 pomegranate
1 lemon

3 tbspn sweet sherry
1 tbspn caster sugar
cream

Dice the pineapple; take the seeds out of the kumquats and slice them thinly. Remove the flesh from the peeled pomegranate and mix it with the pineapple and kumquat. Pour the sherry and lemon juice over and sprinkle on the sugar. Leave to marinate and chill for some hours before serving with cream.

Lichees are obtainable both fresh and tinned, although the 'fresh' lichees are in fact in shells which have dried to brownish black. Freshly picked ripe lichees are red, a little bigger than cherries. The thin skin is hard and scaly and comes away easily from the white fruit when pinched. The tinned fruit are imported in syrup and should be eaten without further cooking.

Fresh lichees can be eaten straight from their skins, or in a

150

syrup made from 4 oz/100 g sugar and $\frac{1}{2}$ pint/3 dl water, heated together. Do not cook the lychees; simply skin them and leave them to soak in this syrup for about an hour before serving.

Limes. Fresh limes look like small lemons and are even sharper, but the juice when sweetened can now be bought in a squeezy container, shaped and coloured like a huge fresh lime. The juice acts in the same way as lemon to stop other fruits, such as apples, from going brown, so can usually be added to fresh fruit salads.

Loquats or Japanese Medlar. A sweet but tart refreshing fruit, which can either be bought in tins or fresh from specialist shops.

Mango. This is a very popular Far Eastern fruit, about the size of a big pear with green skin which turns yellow as the fruit ripens. The flesh is bright orange, close textured and sweet. Mangoes can be eaten raw, but should be chilled or they may have a slightly turpentiney taste. The best way to prepare the fruit is to peel it and then cut the flesh away from the large kernel in slices, and serve in bowls with cream or vanilla ice cream.

Mango Fool

6 mangoes or 1 tin	small carton double cream
sugar to taste	chopped nuts

Peel the fresh mangoes and cut all the flesh from the stones. Put the flesh into a pan with just enough water to stop it burning and cook it until it is tender. Put it through a sieve or blender and when cool add the sugar and whipped cream. Decorate with nuts.

If tinned mangoes are used, do not cook them.

Melons. The three main types are water melon, honeydew and canteloupe. All can be tested for ripeness by very gently pressing at each end. If the melon feels hard, leave it for a day or two to ripen, as there will then be much more juice. A

151

ripe melon gives under the thumb. Melon should be served chilled with the pips scooped out, by itself or with just a sprinkling of caster sugar, and on honeydew perhaps a sprinkling of powdered ginger. Melon is the best of all fruits to serve after a hot curry as it is so refreshing and cool.

Nectarines are smooth-skinned peaches and can be eaten unpeeled fresh, or cooked using any recipe for peaches. Cut the fruit in half and scoop out the stone.

Oranges. Another refreshing fruit to eat after curry either in a fruit salad or just straight from the skin. Some oranges are a little difficult to peel and in that case either chill them in the fridge for an hour, or cover them with boiling water for a few minutes.

Passion Fruit have a sharp tangy taste and can be eaten sprinkled with a little sugar, or added to fruit salads. The fruit are small, round, purplish brown, and do not look particularly appetising, but when cut in half they reveal a bright yellow, green and pink interior. Serve them cut in half on a bed of crushed ice in small bowls and scoop out the flesh with a teaspoon. Passion fruit pulp can also be bought in tins.

Paw Paws or Papaya. The paw paws for sale in this country are small compared to those which can be bought in their native countries. The texture is creamy and close, rather like that of fresh mango, and the taste very slightly peachy with a smokey overtone. The flesh is a nice orange colour. Slice the fruit in half, remove the pippy centre and scoop it from the rind with a spoon. Eat it with a little sugar.

Paw Paw and Passion Fruit Salad

1 paw paw seeded, peeled and diced
2 passion fruit
1 orange peeled and sliced
3 tbspn pineapple pieces

$\frac{1}{4}$ pint/$1\frac{1}{2}$ dl pineapple juice or syrup from a tin
1 tbspn rum
1 lime or 1 tbspn lime juice

Mix together the diced paw paw, flesh from the passion fruit, sliced orange, sliced lime or lime juice, and pineapple pieces. Mix the rum with enough syrup from the pineapple barely to cover the fruit. Or use pineapple juice with extra white sugar. Chill thoroughly before serving.

Peaches. Another marvellous fruit to eat fresh after curry. The best way to peel fresh peaches is to dip them in a bowl of boiling water for 5 seconds, then drain them and put them at once in a bowl of cold water. The skin will peel off in large flakes.

Peach Melba

1 peach per person, fresh or tinned	1 tbspn redcurrant jelly toasted almonds
2 tbspn vanilla ice cream	

Skin the peaches as above, then slice them in half round the crease and remove the stone. Put a spoonful of ice cream in each half and pour over it the previously melted and then cooled redcurrant jelly. Sprinkle on a few roasted and chopped almonds.

Pears. Ripe and juicy pears are best eaten as plain raw fruit, but they can be skinned, cut in half with the pips removed, and lightly stewed for a few minutes, chilled, and then served with chocolate sauce poured over them.

Persimmons. For those who like a very sharp fruit, persimmons can be served straight, with the skin scored in quarters and then peeled back, but most people prefer the fruit with added ice cream or custard. (See also Persimmon Ice Cream page 144).

Pineapples. Slice the leaf and stem off a ripe pineapple and cut it across in slices about $\frac{1}{2}$ inch thick. Cut off the skin and the woody bits with a sharp knife and remove the tough centre core with an apple corer. Arrange the slices in a serving dish and marinate for a couple of hours in liqueur (Cointreau, Grand Marnier) and caster sugar.

Pineapple Salad

1 large tin pineapple pieces   caster sugar to taste
1 apple   1 tbspn Cointreau
2 pears   few drops lemon juice
½ lb / 225 g white grapes

Peel the fruit and seed the grapes; core and slice the apple
and pears, and put with the chopped pineapple pieces in a
large fruit dish. Pour the juices over the fruit. Stir in the
Cointreau. Taste it before adding sugar, as only a very little
will be needed if the apple is sweet. If all the ingredients are
kept in the fridge before preparation, and the salad is served
immediately after being made, the apple will not go brown.
But if they are prepared a little while beforehand and put
to cool in the fridge, add a squeeze of lemon juice to keep
the fruit a bright colour.

Mint and Ginger Drink

4 oz / 100 g fresh mint   1 tbspn lemon juice
½ tspn ground ginger   1½ pint / 9 dl water
3 oz / 75 g sugar

Put the mint leaves with all the other ingredients, and
liquidise them for about 5 minutes. Strain until the liquid
is quite clear and serve over crushed ice. Garnish with a
few sprigs of fresh mint.

Lussi

A very refreshing sweet or salty drink. In hot countries salt is usually added as this helps to counteract salt loss caused by excessive sweating, but to Western tastes, sweet lussi is nicer.

Equal quantities natural yoghurt and fresh milk; to each ½ pint of mixture add:

1 level tspn caster sugar
   (or big pinch of salt)
1 tbspn lemon juice
2 ice cubes

3 or 4 drops of strawberry, raspberry or almond essence

Put all the ingredients together in a blender and give them a quick whisk, or put in a tall jug and beat with an egg beater.

Iced Coffee

1½ pints/9 dl coffee, made
   with either fresh or instant
   coffee according to taste
3 ice cubes

4 drops vanilla essence
4 tbspn vanilla ice cream
whipped cream

Make the coffee fairly strong and allow it to chill in the fridge. Put the coffee in a tall jug with the ice cubes and vanilla essence and beat together with an egg whisk, or electric whisk or blender. Fill tall glasses two thirds full, and add a tablespoonful of ice cream and/or a tablespoonful of whipped cream to the top and serve at once with straws and spoons.

Iced Lemon Tea

juice of $\frac{1}{2}$ lemon per person
cold tea
ice cubes

Put the lemon juice in a tall glass, top up with tea and add two ice cubes. Garnish with a slice of lemon.

Chapter 8

SERVING CURRY, CURRY DINNERS, CURRY PARTIES

Serving Curry

Presentation is very important with all food, and particularly so for curry because by its very nature it tends to be rather mixed up. It has no one striking feature like a salmon dressed up for the table, or a joint of roast pork with crackling, or a roast duckling garnished with orange. Therefore the garnishes and side dishes provide most of the colour. This is why in Thailand and Indonesia fresh fruit is cut and carved into lovely shapes and set up among curries to give the table colour and design. The rice should form a kind of frame or background. It is essential that all the different things be presented on separate dishes and guests allowed to help themselves. Although we do sometimes pile rice on a dish round a curry, this is not really correct, as it is always up to the eater to choose for himself how much rice he wants to take. Sometimes the rice may be served beside the curry on the same big plate or serving dish, but the curry should never be poured over the top of the rice. As mentioned in the section on curry parties, metal dishes and hotplates should be used to keep the food hot, always a problem with curries.

Curry should be eaten with a dessertspoon and fork, but

provide a knife for each guest as many seem lost without one. If there is room at the table, provide each guest with an extra-large side plate as ordinary bread and butter plates can soon be overloaded with odds and ends. I do not like to pile too many different curries and accompaniments and chutneys on my plate at the same time – they run together and flavours become mixed and lost. I would rather put some accompaniments on a big side plate and help myself from that. For a small dinner party there is no reason why dishes should not be kept on central hot plates and each eater encouraged to help himself continually to small portions and to transfer them to his own plate, rather as one does in a Chinese restaurant. One can commit no terrible social blunders; the most sensible way to eat any curry is the way which transfers the food from the serving dishes to your stomach with the least trouble!

Do label everything, even the chutneys and accompaniments, quite clearly, specially with reference to degree of hotness. Thus 'Chicken Pilau, mild', 'Chilli relish, very very hot'. Otherwise, too much of the food will be wasted when your guests find it too hot or too mild for their tastes.

Curry Dinners

As I have said at the beginning of this book there is no reason why you should not serve anything with anything, but it is best to think in terms of balance of dishes when planning a curry menu.

One may start with a cold curry soup, which is fairly light, or with a hot curry soup or chicken mulligatawny which can be a meal in itself, but if you are planning a very special main curry, possibly a pilau or biriani containing rice, then soup is not really necessary, nor is any other 'starter'. However, if you insist upon a starter, then serve something light, half an avocado pear with vinaigrette sauce, or even half a grapefruit.

If the main curry you choose does not contain rice, then serve plain or yellow or saffron rice with it, cooked separately. ½ lb/225 g uncooked rice is plenty for four people.

One cooked vegetable curry is all that is needed with any good meat curry which has plenty of sauce or gravy. Give plenty of choice of accompaniments, from uncooked coolers such as cucumber and yoghurt, sliced banana, to green sambals. Perhaps a home-made hot relish of some kind (hot tomato and chilli) and/or home-made or bought chutneys from mild to very hot. Dahl may be served with any meat or poultry curry. Do not serve rice AND bread; both together are too filling, but serve poppadums and prawn crackers.

With dry curries serve dahls of the consistency of thick soup, or accompanying dishes of vegetables with peanut or coconut sauce. With fish curries serve plenty of rice and lightly cooked vegetables or vegetables in peanut or coconut sauce, or pakoras cooked in batter. Hot soy sauce goes well with fish.

Strips of omelette serve to garnish vegetable and rice dishes, as do slices of hardboiled egg, cucumber, lemon wedges, etc. These add colour as well as taste and bulk.

There are many recipes for suitable desserts in this book. If the curry has been filling, then it is best to serve fresh fruit or fruit salad. Serve richer and more filling 'afters' only if you feel that the early course has not been particularly filling. After a really big curry nothing is better than a water ice or sorbet.

Wine is rather killed by curry and many people prefer iced lager beer, iced lime juice or plain iced water. Iced tea or coffee or lussi are refreshing after a 'hot' meal.

Giving a Curry Party

The difference between a curry party and a curry dinner is that at a dinner everyone is seated round a table and at a party the food is served at a buffet or is set out so that guests can help themselves.

Because all the recipes in this book, except where stated, are for from four to six people according to appetite, it is easy enough just to double up quantities to provide the right amount of food for more people. Hosts always worry that not enough food has been provided and that the food

159

will run out, so the tendency is usually to over – rather than under – estimate the quantities needed.

For a small curry party it may be best to do one really large central dish of meat curry with various vegetable curry accompaniments, and lots of side dishes and chutneys, some rice and bread, poppadums, etc, but variety really is the essence of a good curry party and four main curries at least are recommended, totalling the amount you think is needed for your guests. In other words, if you have sixteen guests, then four main curries each sufficient for four to six people will be ample if accompanied by plenty of side dishes, and at least two vegetable curries. Guests tend to take a little from each main dish rather than more of just one or two dishes. Do NOT provide too much rice; it just will not be eaten because your guests will fill themselves up with the more tasty main dishes. A good pilau or nasi goreng will provide a tasty rice dish, but if you have twenty guests only make enough for ten. A biriani, which has more meat than rice, could be one of the main dishes.

One of the problems of giving a curry buffet is to keep all the food warm. Those fortunate enough to have hotplates or hot cabinets will use them, and the Chinese restaurant type hot plate which has a night light in it is also very useful. The hostess may find herself switching dishes around from table to hot plate to keep them warm. Certainly serve the food in metal dishes if possible, silver entrée dishes, copper or stainless steel dishes retain heat much better than any kind of china. One way round this is not to serve all the hot curries at the same time. This happens in Indonesian restaurants where fresh displays of hot food, always different, are brought to the table throughout the meal. Rather shattering when you have just filled up on one delicious offering to be faced with another which looks even better. However, it is always wise to keep a little of each curry back in a saucepan on the cooker so that it can be quickly reheated and added to a dish on the table which is getting low.

From all this you can see that to run a curry party takes quite a lot of work and organising if it is to be successful:

there is no way that everything can just be put on the table hours before the party. Nevertheless there are many side dishes and accompaniments which can be prepared in advance and set out, and very often the main curries can be made the day before and heated up; in fact many curries are much better for being made that way as the spices continue to be absorbed into and to flavour the food. It is only the crisp things, breads, and batter cooked specialities, that must be absolutely freshly made.

Plenty of liquid should be provided with curries, from jugs of plain ice cold water, to fruit squashes, lime juice and iced lager beer. Wine is really killed by curry and it seems a shame to serve it at the same time. Iced tea or coffee can also be served after a curry meal.

If you have plenty of room, then serve desserts, ices, cheese, etc from another table, or ask your guests to have a short pause for digestion and contemplation while you remove the whole of the first course and spattered tablecloth (curry may stain, so don't use your very best) and start all over again with a fresh cloth and bright and refreshing looking 'afters'. On the whole do not go for rich sweet Indian desserts – they are not usually to our Western taste after too many mixed curries. Cooling things such as fruit salad, plain fruit of various kinds or water ice creams or sorbets which can be brought out of the fridge at the last moment are by far the best.

Contrary to popular belief, curry is NOT indigestible, and many of the most important curry spices and herbs are in fact those used by herbalists and in medicine as digestives and settlers. So there really should not be digestive problems for anyone after a curry meal unless they have made absolute pigs of themselves. The Indian way was to tie a thin silk thread round the belly and to stop eating when that broke! I don't think that such an idea would appeal to most Western curry addicts, but it has its points. It is some of the accompaniments, such as bananas, which may cause indigestion if not eaten slowly.

As for numbers, ten or over would constitute a party, less

than ten would probably be a dinner, so in the paragraphs that follow I am supposing that you have at least fifteen guests and shall suggest dishes which would make a good party table.

Curry Party Menu No. 1

Based on one main dish which will take time to prepare.
For 15 people.
Very simple menu apart from the Birianee.

Lamb Birianee (page 131). Treble quantities.
    Garnish with:
15 Eggs in Turmeric (page 137).
Dahl (page 67). Double quantities.
Curried Green Beans (page 100). Double quantities.
5 bananas (page 103).
Cucumber Cooler (page 104). Treble quantities.
1 poppadum per person (see page 69).
Provide as many bottled chutneys as you have available, including Sweet Mango.
Any other simple accompaniments that you wish to make.

Follow with Fruit Sorbet (page 146). Double quantities will provide a tablespoonful each.
A bowl of fresh apples, pears, oranges or satsumas.

Drink lager beer, or iced lime juice.

Curry Party Menu No. 2

Based on 3 easy curry recipes.
For 15 people.

Meat Balls in Curry Sauce (page 40). Double quantities.
Serve in a ring of plain boiled rice (see page 61) or Saffron
   Rice (page 63). Use 1 lb rice.
Pork Vindaloo (page 59).
Pear, Prawn and Pepper Curry (page 48).
Curried Eggs and Salad (page 50).
1 poppadum per person (page 69).
5 Bananas (page 103).
Green Sambal (page 105). Double quantities.
Yoghurt Relish (page 106). Double quantities.
Spiced Aubergines and Peppers (page 95).
Chutneys: Sweet Mango, Mild Brinjal and Hot Lime or
   Lemon Pickle.

Follow with Grape and Melon Fruit Salad (page 149).
   Treble quantities.

Drink lager beer, iced lime juice or lussi (page 155).

Curry Party Menu No. 3 (Indo-Chinese Style)

A collection of varied dishes in which no particular one is
the main dish.
For 15 people.

Nasi Goreng (page 123). Double quantity.
1 Spring Roll (page 74) per person.
Hot vegetables with peanut sauce (page 124).
Diced Pork in Coconut Sauce (page 81).
Chinese Chicken Curry (page 43). Double quantity.
Steak Sate (page 82). Double quantity.
Bean Sprouts sprinkled with soy sauce (page 67).
Shrimp and Split Pea Savouries (page 107).
Serve with plenty of prawn crackers (page 71).
Sliced Bananas (page 103).
Hot Tomato Relish with Shrimps (page 109).
Spiced Chilli Paste (page 108).

Follow with a dish of Banana Halva (page 142). Triple
quantity, and/or halved Chinese gooseberries (kiwi fruit)
in a dish of crushed ice served with cream, ice cream, or
yoghurt.

Drink lager beer, iced lime juice, or iced tea.

Curry Menu No. 4 (Vegetarian)

Strict vegetarians do not eat eggs, but this collection includes one curried egg recipe.
For 15 people.

Apple Curry Soup (page 55).
15 Eggs in Turmeric with Rice (page 137).
Hot Vegetables with Peanut Sauce (Gado gado) (page 124). Double quantities.
Yoghurt Relish (Raeta) (page 106). Triple quantities.
15 Spring Rolls, omitting prawns and pork or bacon (page 74).
Several plates full of Pakoras using batter No. 2 (page 73) with various vegetables as suggested.
A plateful of Samosas filled with a mixture of potatoes, herbs, onions, and green peas (page 75).
Spiced Aubergines and Peppers (Bughia) (page 95). Double quantities.
Bean Sprouts and Sesame Seeds (page 53).
Green Sambal (page 105). Double quantities.
Plenty of Chutneys.
Spiced Chilli Paste (page 108).

Follow with Sweet Pilau (page 138). Triple quantities.
Banana Halva (page 142). Triple quantities.
Any Fruit Ice Cream.
Any fresh Fruit Salad.

Drink lussi (page 155) or lager beer.

Index

C